Water Before Coffee

Water Before Coffee

Letting Go, Opening Up, and Embracing Life After Pain

Written by Melissa Renee

Book Cover by Alan Hebel / theBookDesigners

Editing by Ellen Tarlin

#1 edition 2026

Evan Carter

1998–2016

The wound of losing you planted the seed for the need to heal.

Preface

Many of us are carrying experiences we have never fully examined.

Not all trauma is loud. Not all of it has a name we feel comfortable saying. Sometimes it is obvious. Sometimes it is something we have minimized for years because it "wasn't that bad." Sometimes it is a collection of moments that shaped how we react, protect ourselves, or make ourselves smaller.

You may not think of yourself as someone who has experienced trauma. You may simply feel tired. Or stuck. Or caught in patterns you cannot explain. You may have grown in many ways and still sense that something remains unsettled beneath the surface.

That is the space this book was written for.

Water Before Coffee is not here to label you or reduce your life to a diagnosis. It is here to help you recognize what has shaped you—your habits, your boundaries, your health, your motivation, your relationships—and to offer a way to rebuild with intention rather than reaction.

Some chapters may feel uncomfortable. Others may feel like relief. You may recognize yourself in pages you did not expect to. Move slowly. Skip ahead if you need to. Return when something feels close to home.

This book includes discussion of difficult subjects, including sexual assault and domestic violence. These topics are addressed with care, but they may be sensitive for some readers. Please read at a pace that feels safe for you.

You do not need a dramatic story to deserve healing. If something changed you, it matters. If something hurt, it counts. If something shaped how you see yourself or the world, it is worth understanding.

You do not have to overhaul your life in a week. You do not have to get everything right. You do not even have to know exactly what you are healing from yet.

Just begin here.

Contents

Chapter 1

Unmasking Trauma
Breaking Free from the Burden

Of all the words we throw around every day, there's one that typically doesn't come up in casual conversation, and it comes with a weight.

Trauma.

It lingers on the edge of our minds, tucked away where it can go unnoticed—until the day comes when you can't push it away anymore. It's an invisible burden we carry, often brushing past the hints of influence it has on our daily lives.

Our instinct is to push it away, thinking that hiding it will prevent us, as well as the people around us, from feeling uncomfortable. We think that if we talk about it openly, admit to it, or even briefly mention it in passing, people will view us differently. Feel sorry for us. We naturally harden our outer shells, convinced that it's better to live this way.

The hard truth is that, in doing this, we're only further damaging ourselves. When we actively move forward in life without addressing our hardships, we lock ourselves in a cycle that prevents us from growth.

True healing begins when you look your trauma in the face. Confront it. Sit with it. Talk about it. Acknowledge it. Accept it.

Don't ignore it.

If you're reading this, then chances are you're beginning to break free. Realizing there is something in your life that is keeping you chained to the ground is no small feat. It's a huge step. It's everything.

If you are healing, on the verge of working through current or past wounds, or even trying to figure out how to guide someone else through their own challenges—this is a courageous act. Deciding to confront the *dark shadow of trauma* requires some serious mental strength.

There are days when this path will feel like a burden. Days when you feel you can't move on. Days when you feel stuck. Days when you just don't understand why. Days when you'll be tested, and days when you'll be lured into pausing this healing journey so you can just get some sleep.

When that happens, you must remember to take one day at a time. One foot in front of the other. Remember the strength it took to take the initial step, and don't move backward. Better days are ahead—you just can't see them yet, and that's okay. That's expected.

Healing allows you to reclaim your future. It allows you to have those peaceful moments without anxiety, and to be able to take a deep breath without feeling a weight on your chest. It allows you to not be triggered by various random events on any given day.

Unhealed trauma does not magically disappear. Despite what you might have been told, not all wounds heal with time. Wounds heal with strength, intention, presence, tears, anger, grief, frustration, stress, and every morning you choose to get up again. And sure . . . you can throw *time* in there if you really want to.

Trauma burrows itself deep into our minds and creates an entirely new map of how we think, feel, and operate. It makes itself nice and comfortable, right at home. It's a freeloader, and it will stay as long as you let it—whether you notice it or not.

In an attempt to protect us, the brain starts to rewire itself. It makes room for its new trauma tenant. It produces higher stress responses, emotional instability, memory loss, and even plain old common-sense cognition errors. It stops trusting things it should trust. It starts feeling insecure and on edge. It keeps you from connecting with others like you normally would because it's trying to protect you.

Trauma rearranges its new home (your brain) to make sure it's nice and cozy. It increases the activity in your amygdala—your internal alarm system—to make sure you sense every possible threat. Especially the nonexistent ones.

It puts you into a state of hyper-awareness, where you can't really tell if something is a true threat anymore. For example, if you've been in a traumatic car accident, your new trauma brain tenant will now panic every time you get into a car. You could simply be trying to get to the grocery store, but that car accident will replay in your mind and cause you to fear danger when the danger isn't there anymore. The car accident is over, but your brain doesn't want you to realize that. It wants to make sure you stay hyper-aware of your surroundings, to prevent the damage from happening again.

Instead of this protecting you, it can make your reality more danger-ous. It can make you overreact in a normal situation or be overly cautious on the road so you become a danger to other drivers. It does the opposite of what it intends to do.

Trauma causes simple everyday stressors (like a sudden burst of noise) to trigger a choking feeling of fear or anxiety. This is exhausting.

Simultaneously, trauma can damage the prefrontal cortex in your brain. This is the region that's responsible for your reasoning, emotional regulation, and decision making (pretty important stuff). When this region becomes less active due to trauma damage, you can probably guess what happens. You respond to emotional events without any form of reasoning. Whether it's the way someone talks to you or a sudden change of plans, you overreact and make decisions based on sudden emotion. You get upset and say, "You are really unreliable and I don't think we should be friends anymore." rather than "Yeah, it *really is* horrible weather today, so I agree we should reschedule."

Trauma can also resize your hippocampus, the part of your brain that handles memory. This can cause flashbacks to a traumatic event that makes you feel like it's happening again in real time. You can become disconnected and struggle with feeling present in your life. It can make you feel like you aren't actually living your day-to-day routine; you're just watching it like a movie.

All of these neurological effects make recovering and healing feel impossible because you feel confused. You can't tell if there's a real threat anymore. You can't remember things. You don't feel present. You feel numb.

Adding insult to injury, continuing to deny the trauma you're carrying can cause your brain to create *not-so-ideal* methods of coping in lieu of proper healing. These methods can get destructive.

For example, maybe it causes you to turn to alcohol, nicotine or other drugs, looking for that "healed" feeling. It could also cause you to self-sabotage (putting in a lot of overtime at work, for instance), self-harm (even worse), or finding sweet, sweet solace in a toxic and abusive relationship.

These might not appear to be coping mechanisms, but they're common trauma responses you might not recognize. They provide temporary relief or distraction, but they don't provide anything close to the long-term healing and growth you need to thrive.

And honestly, they dig you far deeper into your trauma, making it much harder to begin your healing journey once you're finally ready. It's a lot harder to dig yourself out of a ten-foot hole than a two-foot hole.

That's not to say if you're currently reading this from the bottom of a ten-foot hole you dug yourself that there isn't any hope. It might take a bit more willpower and strength, but you can do it.

What's so powerful about healing is that it deals with the past only as much as you want it to. There's no need to dwell on your current situation and sit in disappointment. Healing is about freeing yourself from the patterns that are holding you in place. It's the conscious choice to break the cycle of pain and stillness and make space for growth. It's about happiness.

It's time to take back control of your mind and heart, learn new ways of coping, and create a future no longer controlled by the pain of your past. Healing is a choice. It opens the door to reality and allows you to truly and intentionally *live,* not just exist.

On the other hand, maybe you're the kind of person who thinks you're invincible when it comes to trauma, and you're reading this only because someone bought it for you, or someone important in your life wants you to. Maybe you think you're immune to addiction and unhealthy coping mechanisms because you believe *trauma is just a part of life* and *everyone has to get over it.*

Think again.

Your trauma doesn't create coping mechanisms that are always obvious to pinpoint. Our brains and bodies keep track of everything (whether we want them to or not), and they coordinate with each other in an effort to protect us. If addiction isn't your go-to coping mechanism, maybe your body has resorted to fight-or-flight without you realizing it because you're just so used to it.

Picture this: Someone raises their voice at you, and suddenly, you're seeing red. You can't even hear what they're saying. You can't carry the conversation any further. Maybe you lash out directly at them in a defensive mode, or maybe you retract while panic washes over you and you can't think of anything to say. Your chest tightens, your heart pounds, and an overwhelming urge to escape takes over. You don't care about the conversation anymore; you just want to *get away.*

In that moment, your brain is reacting as if it's in immediate danger. It's not just you being hormonal or moody. You're in fight-or-flight mode and don't realize it. Your brain is telling you you're in immediate danger and need to protect yourself, whether that's by fighting back or running away, when in reality, you're just facing someone who's upset. Sound familiar?

Coping mechanisms (voluntary or not) keep us on high alert and always bracing for the next threat. Even when the painful experience might continue to move further and further into your past, its impact will linger, clouding memories, distorting perceptions, and filling us with self-doubt.

In fact, many people block out entire periods of their lives without realizing it because of one single event where the pain was too great to process. It's common. I, personally, couldn't tell you a single thing about my middle school. Sure, I know the name of it, but I couldn't name a single teacher, remember a single dance, or give you the slightest clue about what I might have been like. Three whole years of my life, just gone. Funny how that works.

Another disappointing aftereffect of trauma is the pure annihilation of your self-trust. It makes you question your thoughts, feelings, and even memories of the event. You alter the narration in your head of what you *know* happened and feel confused, wondering if it was really as bad as you remember or if you aren't remembering it correctly. Worse, you might start thinking you deserved it.

I know what it's like to be locked in your head, cycling through the same thing over and over while trying to get it all to make sense. It can feel isolating. If this is something you identify with, understand this:

your feelings are valid. What happened was real. Its impact is real, and it matters. You matter. You aren't alone.

Working through these truths is quite possibly the hardest part of healing. Healing won't be easy, and it won't happen overnight. It will be a long and gruesome journey that entails confronting things you've been pushing aside.

It will be worth it. The transformation you'll have and the feeling of being yourself again will be worth every ounce of pain. In healing, you trade self-doubt for self-compassion, fear for trust, and suffering for purpose. When all is said and done, you'll start to see yourself not as something your past created but as someone who can grow, get stronger, and prevail.

The best part? As you heal from one wound, you'll find it simpler to face the next. You won't be thrown so far off balance whenever something bad happens. The past will begin to release its grip. You'll be able to understand and recognize emotional wounds for what they truly are, and you won't identify with them anymore.

You'll have a testament to what you have endured to carry with you. You'll know yourself better. You'll start reacting to triggers more and more subtly and clearly. You'll wade through the troubles of life with resiliency, not avoidance.

No two journeys are the same, yet we all carry our burdens. While I'm neither a counselor nor a therapist, I hope to share what I've learned from my own journey.

I'm a woman in my twenties who still watches childhood TV reruns on weekends, gets confused when someone tries to give me verbal directions (like seriously, can we use a GPS?), drinks at least four coffees a day, and works a normal nine-to-five job. However, I've had the *honor* (should we call it that?) of getting a life's worth of trauma dealt to me and have come out the other side all right. My challenges have shaped me, but they don't consume me anymore.

Give yourself permission to confront hard truths. Acknowledge the weight of what you carry. Stand in front of the mirror, take a deep breath, and ground yourself in this moment, because *this* is the start.

It will not be easy. As I said, there will be moments when you feel you are suffocating. The pain is your transformation. By allowing yourself to face it rather than escape, you open a doorway for actual healing.

Incrementally, you will rebuild.

If you met me today, you would not see the weight of my past. My scars are not visible, but they are there. I have lived longer than I could have ever dreamed of, and that's because I didn't give up.

Neither will you.

Chapter 2

Finding Your Presence
Navigating the Silence after the Storm

Experiencing trauma (or a particularly difficult life event) might render your day-to-day life utterly unfamiliar. It's like you've been dropped into a new world where things no longer make sense. What once was familiar becomes alien, and the secure foundation you used to rely on changes, making the most ordinary tasks seem impossible.

One of the first challenges you'll encounter is figuring out how to get your balance back, and attempting to understand where you are in this new and changed life. The sense of being lost, disoriented, or disconnected from reality is common at this stage.

The mind grapples with what's happened, re-enacting moments over and over again as it tries to comprehend them. You'll become tired. You might feel tension. And overall, there's just this sense of unease that follows you around everywhere you go.

It's normal for this phase to feel all-consuming. This is normally where you get the unfortunate "my whole life is ruined" thoughts. Once the intensity and shock start to fade, you're left with a strange numbness.

Feeling numb can be unsettling, like there's a space where emotions once lived. Instead of feeling overwhelmed, you feel hollow and an eerie absence of emotion altogether. You build walls in your mind as you push things away. It distances you from the world around you.

The best way that I can describe feeling numb is to say it's like a dense fog rolling over your mind and muting everything. It's thick. It's hard to see through. It keeps you from moving with purpose.

This emotional detachment never brings comfort, however. It's more of a heavy weight that lingers, making it difficult to engage with life as you once did.

Conversations that felt natural now seem forced. Other people continue with their routines—laughing, working, talking, moving forward—while you remain stuck. It's irritating.

Hobbies and passions that once brought you joy feel meaningless and mundane. It becomes normal to drift through the day in a state of detachment, staring blankly at nothing in particular and losing track of time as thoughts blur.

This disconnection from yourself (and the world) is your mind's way of shielding itself from something too painful or overwhelming to process.

This stillness invites the realization that there is something beneath the surface that needs to be confronted— not a fun feeling. The emptiness you feel in this stage of trauma might seem vast and unfamiliar, but think of it as an opening. Something that needs to be filled. A space for opportunity.

A path exists in this silence that leads toward healing and reconnection; it's just not easy to see. The way forward requires a willingness to explore different approaches until something feels right. Taking even the smallest step toward that pit and reconnecting with yourself is a hurdle, but you can do it with an ounce of hope and the right mindset.

There's a reason the first few weeks (or even months) after a traumatic event are referred to as the aftershock stage.

It's a state of confusion that you have to navigate as the mind and body try to reconcile what the *heck* just happened. It becomes difficult to sleep. You lie awake with racing thoughts before finally dozing off, only to wake up feeling exhausted before you've even gotten out of bed.

Fatigue creeps in, making small irritations intolerable. Patience becomes strained, and coping with the people around you becomes more difficult. Simple tasks now require more energy than they should, and irritability sneaks in from the emotional depletion. Focus is thrown out the window.

Often, this aftershock/numbness state becomes most apparent during social interactions, especially those that once felt natural and now seem foreign.

Sitting with friends and hearing a joke might result in nothing more than a forced half-smile. Laughter might ring out around you while you remain untouched by the joy of the moment. Even celebrations, accomplishments, or moments of shared excitement can feel distant.

Emotionally, the connection is missing, creating a stark contrast between what you understand logically and what you are able to actually feel.

This is when people might also have that "nobody understands" feeling. Numbness is lonely. As solitude sets in, quiet moments with yourself can start to feel especially overwhelming. Early morning hours, long drives, or unexpected lulls in the day can bring a flood of thoughts that refuse to settle.

The mind bounces between trying to make sense of what happened and resisting the pain of fully processing it. This internal struggle only adds to the already existing exhaustion you're facing mentally and physically.

When this emotional overwhelm (or numbness) strikes, breathwork is a powerful and simple tool you can use to ground yourself in the present moment. By consciously shifting your breath, you activate the body's natural relaxation response. It creates a pause in that wave (or lack) of feelings.

There are several effective breathwork techniques that can help restore balance and clarity. Don't be afraid to try different ones until you find what suits your fancy.

Diaphragmatic Breathing (Belly Breathing)

- <u>Focus</u>: Engaging the diaphragm for deep, slow breaths
- <u>When to use</u>: Before sleep, during bouts of anxiety, or in quiet moments of reflection
- <u>How it works</u>: When you engage your diaphragm, you take deep, slow breaths that fill your lungs. This is different from shallow chest breathing, which often happens during stress or anxiety. Diaphragmatic breathing helps your body relax by activating the parasympathetic nervous system, which reduces the fight-or-flight response.
- <u>Benefits</u>: It soothes the nervous system by calming the overactive stress response, lowers heart rate, and reduces blood pressure. This type of breathing improves oxygen flow to the brain and body, helping restore clarity and mental calm. It helps shift from reactive, shallow breathing to a calm, grounded approach, making it easier to manage emotions and stress. Over time, it retrains the body to respond to stress with a sense of calm rather than panic.

Box Breathing

- <u>Focus</u>: Structured breathing pattern
- <u>When to use</u>: When emotions are overwhelming and the mind is scattered

- <u>How it works</u>: The four-part breathing pattern—inhale for six counts, hold for six counts, exhale for six counts, pause for six counts—creates a structured rhythm that helps break the cycle of scattered thoughts. By focusing on counting each breath, the mind is drawn away from the chaos of overwhelming thoughts and emotions, allowing it to focus on the present. This method also triggers the vagus nerve, promoting relaxation.

- <u>Benefits</u>: Box breathing helps restore emotional balance and mental focus by providing a simple but powerful tool to anchor the mind. It reduces the physiological signs of stress, such as rapid heartbeat and shallow breathing, and shifts the body out of the fight-or-flight mode. This leads to greater emotional control, clarity, and a sense of groundedness, especially during moments of intense emotional distress.

Alternate Nostril Breathing (*Nadi Shodhana*)

- <u>Focus</u>: Balancing the body's energy
- <u>When to use</u>: When feeling anxious, mentally foggy, or emotionally unsettled
- <u>How it works</u>: By gently closing off one nostril at a time while inhaling and exhaling, this practice activates both the left and right sides of the brain, promoting balance. The strategy alternates nostrils to help release energy blockages in the body and mind. The even, rhythmic breathing helps harmonize the body's energy, which can become imbalanced during moments of emotional upheaval.

- <u>Benefits</u>: Alternate nostril breathing promotes mental clarity and reduces feelings of anxiety, stress, or mental fog. It calms the sympathetic nervous system, activating the parasympathetic system, inducing relaxation. This technique enhances focus and reduces mental clutter, making it easier to center yourself during emotionally turbulent times. It also harmonizes the nervous system, promoting a steady, grounded state.

Kapalabhati Breath (Skull Shining Breath)

- Focus: Energizing and releasing emotional tension
- When to use: When feeling weighed down by emotional stagnation or mental heaviness
- How it works: This technique involves quick, forceful exhalations through the nose while the inhales are passive. The exhale stimulates the abdominal muscles, activating the lower part of the lungs and pushing out stale air, which creates space for fresh oxygen. This process helps to clear the respiratory system and invigorate the mind. It also helps break through emotional stagnation, physically clearing out tension in the body.
- Benefits: Kapalabhati breath is energizing, increasing oxygen flow to the brain, sharpening mental clarity, and enhancing focus. It helps release pent-up emotions and clears away emotional heaviness. The fast exhalations help release built-up tension, providing a sense of mental renewal and emotional clarity. This technique also promotes better digestion and circulation, giving both the body and mind a sense of rejuvenation.

Conscious Connected Breathing (Circular Breathing)

- Focus: Unbroken, steady flow of breath
- When to use: When emotions feel stuck or when processing trauma

- <u>How it works</u>: In this technique, you breathe in and out in a continuous, connected rhythm, without pausing between inhalations and exhalations. This unbroken flow of breath creates a steady, soothing rhythm that helps the body release pent-up emotions. As you breathe, the practice encourages the release of trapped emotions, allowing feelings to move through the body rather than becoming trapped.

- <u>Benefits</u>: Conscious connected breathing helps release deeply held emotions and unresolved trauma by breaking down the barriers that prevent emotional processing. The continuous breath pattern allows emotional energy to flow freely, promoting healing. It calms the nervous system and restores emotional balance. By focusing on the breath, this technique helps quiet the mind, leading to greater inner peace, emotional stability, and clarity.

These breathwork techniques are more than just stress relievers. They offer serious benefits by improving emotional regulation, physical relaxation, and mental clarity. They aren't going to solve all your problems, but they can be used as a stepping-stone to becoming present again and help you navigate that aftershock. With patience and practice, you'll see how they can shift your body and mind back toward a state of balance and calm.

It's frustrating how trauma has a way of stealing and transforming the simplest parts of your life—turning once effortless tasks into overwhelming obstacles. You can feel like you aren't *used to* anything anymore.

Getting out of bed feels like climbing a mountain. Taking a shower requires energy you no longer have, and even responding to a message or answering a call can feel daunting when your mind is mired in exhaustion.

On top of everything, overstimulation easily compounds the struggle. The constant barrage of notifications, the endless scrolling, and the noise of daily life make everything feel loud. It's heavy and intrusive, and your nervous system is already in overdrive.

Maybe you try to cook dinner, but the blaring television, barking dog, and humming appliances make it unbearable. Even these small, everyday sounds can feel suffocating when your mind is already overwhelmed. Your brain is doing its best to process your day, but when it's bombarded with too much input, it shuts down.

You might sit in front of a meal, unable to eat, or you might find yourself mindlessly consuming food in search of comfort. In these moments, too, breathwork can serve as your anchor and help you regain a bit of control over your day.

Rather than forcing yourself to push through exhaustion and overwhelm, breathwork invites you to pause what you're doing and find stillness. With each breath, you create your own space to feel and process things without feeling like you're drowning.

When the world feels chaotic and out of your control, returning to the simplest thing that you *can* control—your breath—offers a moment of peace and clarity.

Breaking through that paralysis feeling of trauma requires patience and gentle, intentional effort. Large changes might feel overwhelming, but focusing on what I like to call micro-priorities (small, mini tasks) can help you to regain a sense of control.

Micro-priorities aren't big gestures meant to change your life overnight. Instead, they're simple and deliberate actions that serve as small reminders that progress and movement are possible, no matter how stuck you feel. They help give you back your sense of stability.

Making the bed, drinking a glass of water, or even just stepping outside for a breath of fresh air are all little acts of defiance against your aftershock. In moments like these, you remind yourself that you are still here and still capable of taking action. Over time, these small tasks create ripples of momentum that you can carry with you throughout your daily motions.

Micro-priorities allow you to have a task that has a timed beginning and end, without the pressure of perfection or the fear of having to do something for an extended period.

That mountain of laundry doesn't seem so daunting when you're not forcing yourself to complete the whole thing but, rather, you're telling yourself, "I will set a timer for ten minutes, and then I will be done." This way, instead of avoiding the task for a week, you get it done in two or three days by chipping away at it little by little.

Other tasks that might benefit from a ten-minute timer are things like dishes, straightening up a room in your house, watering the garden, organizing the fridge or pantry, and even wiping down surfaces.

Ten minutes. That's all you need to start to get a grasp on things again.

These timed sessions are gentle checkpoints that can give you a sense of completion without stealing too much of the energy (physical and mental) you don't currently have to begin with. They create a routine of movement and rest, prevent quick burnout, and keep things from piling up too much.

Once you get in the habit of using micro-priorities, you'll start to regain a sense of your footing. Even those around you might begin to notice. Friends and family might prod a little bit and ask you how you're doing to see if you're open to conversation. They see your inner world being put together again, and they assume that means you're better.

At this point, their asking might be well-intentioned and come from a place of care and concern, but it will probably still feel a bit overwhelming or frustrating. Attention can make you feel vulnerable and exposed. You might not be ready to put your pain into words, and having an open discussion might cause you to confront emotions that you have been trying to keep at bay.

Not to mention, you probably don't even understand those emotions yet. Being open to discussion means pulling back a curtain before you've had the chance to make sense of what is behind it. It's like having someone knock on your front door and walk right into your house when you aren't even dressed or expecting company.

Deciding whether to open up or keep things to yourself is its own challenge. The thought of sharing feels uncomfortable. What if no one understands? What if sharing makes everything worse? What if people see you differently?

The fear of judgment, or the fear of accidentally saying too much or too little, can be paralyzing. Even acknowledging the weight of your experience feels like a risk, as if saying it might make it more real.

Luckily, at this stage in your healing, you don't need to force yourself to have those conversations yet. Right now, what's most important is that you not jump ahead and just continue the inner work of getting back to your own routine and becoming present.

Be ready and confident enough to politely let someone know that you're not ready to discuss anything yet. Saying something like, "Hey, I understand you care and that you want to be here for me, but right now I'm just not ready to talk about anything yet" is perfectly acceptable. Friends and family can still be there for you simply by being present and acknowledging that you have a weight on your shoulders. Having patience is huge.

If someone starts to get pushy with you, don't be afraid to set a boundary by telling them that when you are ready to talk about it, *you* will come to *them*. This is a nice way of saying "Please don't ask again." Your pain and trauma are not theirs to explore until you're ready, and if they are pushing you, they don't have your best interest in mind.

Being mindful of how you engage with others can also help you stay grounded. When you're with people, let go of any mental checklists of things you need to do or think you might be better off taking care of. Focus on being fully present with them, listening, and interacting as much as you can. This will help to keep a strong connection with the people around you, even when there may or may not be a two-ton elephant in the room. During gatherings, you can step away into the bathroom and do some breathing exercises to regain your presence if you need, and don't be afraid to be the first to leave. Just showing up matters.

Another hurdle you're going to face is emotional triggers. In moments when you feel triggered, it's helpful to have additional self-care activities that promote presence. When I felt triggered, I was far from being present. I was anxious, my mind was racing, I was emotional, and I typically stared into space for an extended period of time.

Something I found helpful when I was in those "freeze" moments was to engage in constant inner narration. Instead of letting my mind go blank (to keep racing thoughts at bay), I silently narrated everything I was doing—literally—whether it was thinking, *I'm walking to my car* or *I'm making breakfast* or *I'm pouring a cup of coffee and then I'm going to sit on the couch*, the inner commentary brought me back to the present.

Every mindless thing I was doing I was now describing to myself as if I was showing it to a toddler. It might sound silly or tedious, but it helped to keep me from slipping into autopilot. It brought purpose and awareness to everything I was doing and filled up my mind with verbiage so there was no room left for spiraling or overthinking.

As you use these techniques in your daily life, you'll begin to notice little changes in yourself. Trauma, once so overwhelming, recedes into the background, making room for little moments of happiness to begin to creep back in. A simple smile at a stranger or a peaceful moment of calm are all clues that healing is taking place.

Another technique to help you ease back into reality is to create a space where you can process your emotions and think about things without external pressure. A quiet, dedicated area you can retreat to in order to reflect or pause.

This might look like a corner of your room, a cozy chair, or even your car. It's a dedicated space for just you, free from expectation or performance. In this place, you aren't required to explain yourself or make sense of anything. It's just a sanctuary, a safe spot.

In order to make this space truly restorative, fill it with items that help bring comfort and calm: soft lighting, a warm blanket, an essential oil diffuser or candle, even some books— sensory items that can generate feelings of ease.

Keeping the space free of clutter is important, too. Clutter equals stress. Each time you enter this space, you want it to serve as a reminder that this is a time to pause, a break from the madness of the outside world, not a reminder that you need to clean.

This is where you can exhale completely. Relax your jaw and your shoulders. Sit with your emotions without worrying about interruption or questioning.

The more you return to this space, the more it will become an anchor for you. Pairing it with small rituals like reading or writing can make it feel even more sacred.

These moments of peace the space will give you (no matter how brief they are) will provide a sense of stability. They are a place for you to gather yourself, let go, and reconnect before you head back out into whatever life will throw your way that day.

If you're looking for something a bit more productive that can help you navigate numbness, one of the most effective things you can do is journal. Journal, journal, journal.

Writing down your thoughts and feelings, whether in a true physical journal or in the notes of your phone, is a powerful way to process your emotions and track your growth. Putting your experiences into words and writing them down can bring you clarity about what you're processing.

Even better, a journal serves as your own personal record. Every moment you choose to document can reveal patterns in your emotions, routines, and mindsets that might otherwise go unnoticed. Over time, your journal entries become a roadmap.

It's helpful to be able to look at past journal entries as a reminder of the progress you've made.

Maybe you're feeling stuck, like you can't heal or haven't made much progress, but when you look at a journal entry from three or four weeks ago, you'll see how things have already changed. Or maybe two years later, when you're having another challenge, you can look back at your entries and compare your healing then to your healing now. You can show yourself what to expect and how long your healing might take.

Journaling allows you to witness your own resilience. You can recognize recurring challenges and celebrate victories both big and small. Maybe you reflect on your journal and see that just two weeks ago, you were barely able to eat three meals a day because you were so depressed, but now you find yourself remembering to pick up dinner on the way home. Small progress is mighty.

Be present with your experience, not just because it allows you to actually face your feelings, but it also prevents you from covering up those feelings with distraction and avoidance.

Your mind resorts to numbing strategies because it is trying to cope. Whether that's mindless scrolling, working yourself to exhaustion, or even self-sabotage, they are all last-ditch efforts to escape pain. These behaviors are expected but should be temporary, and it's up to you to actively change them. Choose not to deepen your wound.

Avoidance looks like an easy way out, but it has a high price. What begins as a form of self-defense turns into self-defeat. Emotional outbursts can strain relationships, and dysfunctional behaviors become patterns that seem impossible to break. The longer the pain is bottled up, the longer it simmers, affecting everything you do, from thinking, to decisions, and especially interactions.

Sooner or later, all burdens need to be addressed. If you don't choose when to address them, they'll choose for you. Spoiler alert: they will pick the most inopportune and undesirable times, like when you've just lost your job, or your car breaks down or you're two-hundred dollars short on rent. When you need to focus your energy a current issue, your past will creep up on you and say "Hey! Don't forget about me! I'm still here, unprocessed!" and dogpile you until you feel like there is no solution to anything at all.

Through the course of your struggles remember that simply being alive is an achievement. It can be easy to forget that it takes courage to continue to live after something has shaken you to your core. As miserable and blunt as that sounds, it's the truth for many people. If the only thing you did today was make it through, that's still a display of resilience. We're starting at the base level here. Seriously.

Reflect on where you were when your trauma first occurred. Think back to those early days that had so much panic, disbelief, and despair. It probably felt like recovery was way out of reach.

Yet, over time, the sharp edges of these emotions might have softened, and you're likely already finding your own ways to cope, even in small doses. Rather than fixating on the end goal of healing, allow yourself to be present and celebrate each step forward.

When all else fails, allow me to introduce you to *the art of doing nothing*. If you don't have the energy for breathing exercises or journaling, and you don't want to set a ten-minute timer to work on something . . . seriously, do *nothing*.

The art of doing nothing is not about neglecting responsibilities or staying stagnant; it's about allowing yourself to just exist. Exactly as you are. Right now. It's not laziness; it's an intentional choice to step away from the pressure of productivity. It's slowing down and allowing your body to naturally heal itself for a moment. Sleep. Breathe. Rest.

At first, the art of doing nothing might feel uncomfortable. Your mind might race with thoughts about all the things you should be doing. You might feel bored. That's okay. What's important about these moments of stillness is that answers to your own questions might just appear. When you aren't forcing your brain to focus on everything going on, it might start to finally come up with solutions to all of your "what if" questions. Maybe you'll feel a sense of calm.

This is about getting to the baseline of being present.

Becoming comfortable with doing nothing can help you to break free from the "next thing" mentality, in which you're constantly trying to make time move faster and worrying about getting things done.

Take a deep breath, close your eyes, and slowly exhale. When you open your eyes, notice your surroundings. Where are you? How many windows do you see? Is anyone else in the room? What time is it? When was the last time you ate?

Close your eyes again and listen to the sounds around you: the distant hum of traffic, the ticking of a clock, the TV, or maybe even the sound of your own inhaling and exhaling.

These small, seemingly insignificant details ground you in the present moment, remind you that you are here. You are safe. You are alive.

Remember, the future that you're working toward won't fully unfold until you give your healing the attention it needs. Time keeps moving forward, and that future will come on its own without you needing to rush it. By focusing on restoring yourself now, you'll be even more prepared to embrace that future when it arrives, showing up as the strongest and most complete version of yourself that you can possibly be.

Chapter 3

Harnessing Acceptance

Your Path to Self-Reclamation and Renewal

Stepping into the present after trauma is like emerging from deep water, gasping for air in a world that feels foreign. After spending so much time disconnected and trapped in the fog of numbness, there is a fragile uncertainty in finally feeling human again.

With that clarity comes the weight of what was lost, the sharp reality of what happened, and the undeniable truth that life will never be exactly as it was.

This is where the real work begins: accepting your truth.

Acceptance does not mean approving of what happened or pretending it no longer hurts. It is not minimizing your experiences or forcing yourself to get over it and move on, either.

True acceptance is the process of making peace with the fact that your trauma exists and that it has shaped you, but it does not define you. Acceptance is the active decision to stop running from your past and instead learn how to carry it with strength, grace and dignity.

Let's paint a picture. It's a leisurely Sunday afternoon, and you're brunching with your two best friends, soaking in the warmth of good company and perhaps some bottomless mimosas. Laughter spills across the table as you swap stories, catching each other up on life's latest twists, work drama, family chaos, and of course, the juicy gossip. As you animatedly recount how your sister's ex-fiancé was cheated on, you notice a subtle shift.

The friend to your left, who was engaged just moments ago, has suddenly fallen quiet, their expression clouded with something unspoken. After some gentle prodding and a flood of concerned questions, they finally admit the truth: they've been cheated on multiple times and have never fully healed from it.

They go on to reveal something even heavier: they believe they were the problem. In their mind, their past controlling tendencies suffocated the relationship, and they've convinced themselves that their actions caused everything.

Now, put yourself in this moment. How do you respond? Would you lash out, scolding them for being ridiculous? Would you shame them into silence, causing them to feel silly or unheard?

Of course not.

You soften, offering reassurance without hesitation. You remind them that they were young, still learning, and that love doesn't come with conditions of perfection. You'd insist that someone else's betrayal was a reflection of their own personal choices, not your friend's worth.

If I were in this situation, I would probably feel sorry for my friend. I would tell them it's easy to focus on what you might have done wrong in search of answers. I would express how proud I am of them for admitting this and encourage them to be a bit more gentle and self-trusting.

Now, let's step away from this dramatic hypothetical and return to reality.

The heart of the matter is this: the kindness, patience, and understanding you would offer a friend in pain is the same grace you owe yourself.

Too often, we hold ourselves to impossible standards. We believe that if we had just done something different, been better, been less this, been more that, we could have prevented our own suffering.

This self-punishment for something unpreventable is like a cement block chained to your feet when you are trying to swim.

You have to stop.

You deserve to fully process your experiences, to learn from them without shame, and to give yourself the space to heal. That doesn't mean ignoring the pain or pretending it never happened; it means embracing the truth of what *was* while allowing yourself to move forward.

Blame has no place in healing, and regret will only keep you stuck in a past you cannot change. What you *can* change is how you choose to accept your story. The way you embrace your past will shape your entire path toward healing. Will you meet yourself with compassion, or will you stand in your own way? The choice is yours.

The first thing I suggest might sound silly, but it can open the door to acceptance for you.

Write a letter. A goodbye letter, to be specific.

This goodbye letter is you saying goodbye to the life you expected. Writing a goodbye letter to that version of you—the life you intended to have before your trauma occurred—might sound depressing or counterintuitive. It might seem harsh to say goodbye to something that hasn't had the chance to happen yet.

The reality is, we all have life plans. We've all held a vision in our minds of how things might look tomorrow, next week, next month, or even a year from now. Things like where we'll live, what job we'll have, what our bank accounts will look like, what our mental state might be, and who will surround us. It's natural. You might not sit down and write out all your life plans physically on a mood or dream board, but the vision is there in your subconscious. And your subconscious probably wasn't expecting or considering that trauma might derail your plans.

Now you're left with a weird feeling of mourning or incompletion that maybe you can't put your finger on yet, but it's there.

I'm not saying your future can't be bright and wonderful and contain all kinds of amazing things—I'm just saying it might be different from what you expected. As the saying goes, "Man plans and God laughs." That also applies to trauma: loss, abuse, injury. You thought you knew what your world would look like today, and it's completely different. You can still have amazing things in your life, but it's important to acknowledge that things won't be as you thought.

Writing this goodbye letter will help you acknowledge this while honoring the strength you have gained. In this letter, you can express your grief while opening the door to a new chapter you might otherwise have not imagined.

To begin, find a quiet space where you can write without interruption, where you don't have to worry about someone reading the letter over your shoulder or catching part of it as they walk by, a place where you can process the emotions of the letter (sadness, anger) without fear of judgment.

Grab a pen and paper, or open your Notes app on your phone, or even dictate it to a voice memo. Set the intention that this letter is a means of closure, *not* a sign of defeat.

Start by acknowledging the life you thought you would have with all the dreams, aspirations, and expectations that seemed so clear to you. Let yourself fully *feel*. Write about the things you imagined. Write about the things that are no longer possible and why they aren't. Write about the events that will never come to be or the milestones that now feel distant. Express your sorrow, and don't try to make it sound "right." This is just for you.

Next, shift your focus slightly. After acknowledging the loss and change, it's time to say goodbye. Acknowledge that the person you are now might never fully align with the person you once thought you would become.

Write something like *I have to say goodbye to the life I imagined, the one that didn't include this pain.*

Saying goodbye allows you to release the hold that these expectations had on you and frees you from the sadness or anger that might come with wanting things to turn out differently.

And remember, I am not telling you to say goodbye to your hopes and dreams. I'm not telling you to lose your ambitions or stop striving for a better future. This is about saying goodbye to the life that existed before this trauma and the version of yourself that didn't carry this weight.

As you continue, give yourself permission to grieve. Describe the specific ways in which the trauma has shaped your life. Name the things that hurt the most. This is the emotional labor of accepting what happened during a *designated time*, and it prevents you from accidentally realizing the emotional labor of trauma in the middle of the grocery store and laying it all out on the clerk who's ringing up your items.

Finally, close the letter with a declaration of acceptance. You can write something like, *I acknowledge what has happened, and I choose to release the version of my life that no longer fits. I will carry forward with the wisdom I have gained, even though it came from pain. I will honor this new life, and make space for the new and adjusted dreams and possibilities that are heading my way.*

Once your letter is complete, take a moment to reflect on what it represents. This is a symbolic act of acceptance and closure. It marks the point at which you stop fighting what you cannot change and embrace what is real. You are making peace with what was lost, and in doing so, you are opening yourself up to what can be. This letter isn't for you to share with anyone. It's for you, and you alone. If it feels right, you might choose to burn it (my preference), bury it, or keep it safe as a reminder for when you need to take control again and reread it.

Unfortunately, no amount of wishing or regret or tears can rewrite the past. You cannot turn back time to undo what happened, to save someone, to protect yourself, or to make a different choice. There's no way to go back and make a left turn instead of a right, unsend a text, pick up a phone call, or stay home that night. No matter how many times you replay the *what-if*s in your mind, your experience is unchangeable. You have to realize that.

What you *can* change is how you carry it. Instead of allowing these thoughts to weigh you down with guilt or regret, you have the power to shift your perspective. Acknowledging the past for what it is instead of trying to rewrite it is difficult but entirely possible. It's so important to remember that your story is still being written, and you are not bound to remain in the chapters that brought you pain. It's simply a matter of turning the page.

In some cases, acceptance might also come through forgiveness—particularly toward those might have played a role in your pain. Forgiving someone does not excuse harmful actions or invalidate your feelings. Forgiveness will allow you to release the grip that resentment has on your heart—not for their benefit but for your own peace. Forgiveness also does not mean we are opening doors for someone to harm us again; it's just simply letting go.

When you adamantly choose to not forgive someone because of how they may have disrespected or treated you, you are only giving them further power.

The desire for closure after a painful event is a natural response to the lingering questions and emotions that often remain unresolved.

Questions like *why would they do this* or *what was really going on* or *what were they struggling with* are expected responses. The mind desperately craves understanding. We hope that by piecing together the details, everything will finally make sense, and we'll understand why something has happened.

It's easy to believe closure will bring relief and offer a sense of finality that allows you to move forward. In some situations, addressing what happened directly with the person involved might seem like the only way to find peace.

However, before taking that step, it's important to consider whether reopening the conversation will truly provide the resolution you are seeking or if it will only prolong the pain.

Not every situation will grant the kind of closure you're looking for. The person who caused you harm might not acknowledge the impact of their actions, offer a meaningful apology, or take responsibility. They might react defensively, blame you, or try to invalidate your feelings or memories. This can not only be confusing, but it also deepens the wounds you are trying to heal.

Walking into any conversation with expectations of how the other person should respond can set you up for further disappointment. If discussing the past with someone feels necessary and like the only way you can move forward, just brace yourself. Prepare for the possibility that they might not give you what you need, but do not allow that to derail your progress.

Before reaching out, reflect on your intentions. Ask yourself whether hearing their perspective or expressing your feelings will truly—and I mean *truly*—help you heal. If the motivation stems from the desire for them to finally validate your pain or understand you, it might be best to reconsider. True closure comes from within, not from someone else's words or actions. The need for external validation can keep you trapped in a cycle of waiting for something that might never come.

Finding acceptance without receiving closure from another person is challenging but entirely possible, and often the best option. Writing a letter expressing everything you wish you could say, even if you never send it, can provide a sense of relief. Talking through your feelings with a trusted friend or therapist or even journaling about your experience can help untangle the emotions that feel unresolved.

Changing your perspective from getting closure from someone else to getting closure from within allows you to regain control of your healing. Some wounds will never receive an explanation, some people will never provide an apology, and some situations will always remain unfair.

Another way to help you gain closure is to close your eyes and picture your pain as something outside yourself. What does it look like? Does it have a shape, a color, a presence? Perhaps it feels heavy like a stone, jagged like glass, or dark like a shadow.

Now, consider giving it a name. Not necessarily a literal one (though you can if it helps) but a word that represents its essence. Maybe it is *the weight* or *the storm*. Maybe it's *echo* because it keeps replaying memories. You can even name it Brad if you want; I'm not judging. Whatever you choose, this name allows you to recognize your pain without fully identifying with it. This allows you to begin to separate it from yourself and continue working on accepting it.

Now that your pain has a name, speak to it. This might seem strange at first, but imagine it as something that has been holding on to you, waiting to be acknowledged, following you around right at your heels, and not giving you any privacy. Maybe you want to ask it why it's still here, or tell it to leave. Ask it what it is trying to prove to you or teach you. Draw a line in the sand and make it stand on the other side, creating a clear separation.

Now, send it away. Imagine shooing it away gently but firmly. Picture placing it in a box and setting the box down. Watch it float down a river, dissolve in the wind, or even throw it as hard as you can into the ocean. If the pain returns (as it sometimes will), remind yourself you have already spoken to it and told it you don't need it anymore. You do not have to re-explain yourself to it, reason with it, or pick it back up.

You can greet it, recognize it for what it is, and even give it the understanding you deserve—but then you must learn to let it continue to pass. Step out of its pathway, and keep moving along without it, like an ex-boyfriend you might accidentally run into at the grocery store—it's awkward, you know why it doesn't make you feel good, and you choose to go about your day instead of rekindling the relationship in aisle 3.

Now that you've theoretically eliminated your pain stalker named Brad, you can welcome something new, a reminder object to serve as a tangible representation of your journey toward acceptance and the space you no longer have to carry it. This object will serve as a physical anchor for you that grounds you in the truth of what you have overcome and the strength you continue to build. Unlike fleeting or random thoughts and emotions that come in waves on this journey, this reminder object will remain steady and offer reassurance in moments of doubt or difficulty. You could also think of it as a ward of some sort that keeps the pain from getting too close to you again. Pepper spray for Brad.

Choosing the ideal object is the fun part. It's a careful and personal matter as well. Maybe this reminder object is something you already own or something you obtained around the time of the event. If you don't have anything in mind, don't worry. Something will come to you.

To find your reminder object, begin by reflecting on what brings you a sense of peace and strength. Some people choose a piece of jewelry like a ring or pendant they can wear daily as a quiet affirmation. Others prefer something small enough to carry—like a stone, key, or coin—something they can keep in their pocket or hold in their palm when they need grounding. If nature speaks to you, consider selecting a shell, feather, or even a smooth rock, maybe even something from the location where your trauma happened. If you're like me, you might choose something a little more permanent, such as a tattoo or permanent jewelry. Lastly, if you want something brand-new with no association to anything that has happened, visit a store or market with an open heart and mind, allowing an object to choose you.

Once you have your object, take a moment to assign it meaning. Hold it in your hands and think about why you chose it. Let it represent a promise to yourself to accept, heal, and move forward. You can even speak words of affirmation over it, like "this holds my strength." By doing this, you transform it from an ordinary object into something sentimental and significant, something that will always carry the energy of your journey.

In my experience, I leaned toward permanent jewelry that would ultimately be removed. My life goal was to move to my happy place—a little town on the East Coast (somewhere that someone in my past told me I would never make it). To represent this, I got a permanent bracelet that had a pearl. Moving to this place was such a big deal to me because it would be me finally living my dreams for myself, getting away from the places that caused me trauma, and honestly, being free. I looked at it on my wrist every day for almost three years straight. Once I moved, I cut the bracelet off, symbolizing reaching my milestone and being free from this weight I carried. I was healed and starting over fresh, on my own terms. It was incredibly impactful, and I will never forget the day I stood in the mirror and cut off that bracelet. I didn't need that protection and motivation anymore.

Deciding where to keep your reminder object depends on how you want to use it. If you find yourself needing frequent reassurance, you can keep it in your pocket or your purse, or even on a chain around your neck. This allows you to quickly grab it whenever you feel that pain start to creep in.

If you see it as a marker of progress rather than as something to carry, you can place it somewhere like your nightstand, a bookshelf, or next to a framed photo that represents your growth.

Some even choose to keep it tucked inside a journal or a small box, taking it out only during moments of reflection. However you decide to keep it, just ensure it is easily accessible when you need it most.

When you feel yourself slipping into old patterns like doubt, grief, depression, or even denial, reach for your reminder object. Let it remind you that you are not where you started and that you are actively working toward acceptance.

In these difficult moments, do your best to take a deep breath, grip the object, and affirm your resilience. Over time, simply seeing or touching it will be enough to center you, bringing you back to the truth that you are moving forward, even when it might not always feel like it.

As time passes, your relationship with this object might change. One day, you might realize you no longer need it the way you once did because the strength it symbolized has become a part of who you are. When that moment comes, you can choose to pass it on, place it somewhere sacred, or get rid of it (like I did with cutting off the bracelet) knowing that it has fulfilled its purpose.

In letting go of your object, there might be a strange sense of grief. I found myself crying when I cut my bracelet off. It's like you have this thing that has been there with you through all the tears and emotions and waves, and now you don't need it anymore. It's normal to have a connection with it. This connection is representative of the person you were when you clung to it for stability. Whether you decide to hold on to it or eventually release it, it will remain a testament to your courage, your healing, and your power to accept what once felt unbearable.

This feeling of grief can catch you off guard. It's a sadness for what happened but also an aching sorrow for what has been lost, including the version of you that existed before the trauma. It's disorienting when you start to realize that healing is not simply moving forward but also coming to terms with the fact that you're a different person now.

This feels personal, almost like losing a dear friend. The version of you that was fearless, carefree, and unshaken by doubt might now feel like a distant memory. There might be a longing for the person who once moved through life without any hesitation, who trusted easily, and who never second-guessed their decisions. It's hard when you're yearning for that past self. It's normal to want to have back the personality that embraced life with wide-eyed excitement and chased adventure without fear.

The weight of trauma can make it feel as if that person has been taken away, leaving behind someone who is more of a shadow: guarded and careful. When you find yourself in these confusing waves of emotion, a step forward to acceptance and moving past it all can be to write yourself a truth statement.

The first step in writing a truth statement is allowing yourself to face what happened without minimizing, avoiding, or distorting it. The goal is not to relive the pain but just to state the reality of your experience as clearly and honestly as possible. In doing this, you remind yourself why you are different now and why you feel that grief.

Denial often keeps us trapped in an unclear or softened version of events, making acceptance harder.

Start by writing a single and simple sentence that answers the question *What is the point-blank truth about what happened to me?* Keep it simple and direct, and say it in a way that gives you your power back. Instead of writing *I went through something difficult*, be more specific. You can say, *I was betrayed by someone I trusted* or *I experienced a traumatic event that changed my life*. Next, replay the event on your piece of paper exactly as you remember it. Take your time. It's okay if you don't remember it all clearly or if things seem out of order. What's important is that it's specific to your experience. Writing it down removes the ambiguity and allows you to acknowledge your experience with clarity.

There should not be anyone around you to tell you it happened differently, or to remind you of something that was said. This is just for you and the memories you recall.

Once you have the raw truth written, take a deep breath and sit with it. Notice any discomfort and any urge to soften the words. If denial creeps in, remind yourself that the truth is not going to change, whether you want to acknowledge it or not. We're not trying to judge the writing or make it more palatable; you are just trying to write the truth.

Now that we have the truth written from your hurt point of view, write it again but in a way that frames you as a survivor, not a victim. Instead of *I was abandoned and left to deal with everything alone*, try *I was strong enough to handle myself the best that I could and find a way out*. The idea of doing this is to shift your feeling from helplessness to resilience.

After rewriting your words, read the statement out loud. How does it feel? Does it reflect the truth about what happened and your ability to rise above it? If you still feel weighed down or feel like it doesn't seem right, continue adjusting it to incorporate small victories. For example, if you wrote *I am still struggling every day to accept what happened*, shift it slightly to *I am learning how to accept what happened*. The truth does not have to be rigid or hopeless; it can hold both the weight of your past and the possibility of your future.

As a final step, write your truth statement in its strongest form. Let it be a declaration of what you have lived through and what you are becoming. Keep this statement somewhere visible, whether in a journal, on a note in your phone, or even spoken as a daily affirmation.

While you might never return to the exact version of who you once were, that doesn't mean you are any less whole. Growth after trauma brings new depth, wisdom, and resilience that was not there to begin with. The old you is still there; it is just a softened version that moves forward with greater awareness and self-compassion. You are becoming someone who has been shaped by their experience but is still wholly capable of joy, hope, and love.

This journey of acceptance is not just a mental process; it's also connected to the body. Emotional pain and trauma often manifest physically in the way we hold ourselves. There is most likely tension in your muscles, shallowness in your breath, or the instinct to withdraw from touch or movement. During this process, it's important for you to also do the work to reconnect with this area of yourself.

Take a moment to stop what you're doing and tune into your body. Find a peaceful space where you can focus. Close your eyes and pay attention to your breath. Notice the way the air moves in and out of your body. Does it feel shallow, or are you able to get a full, deep breath in? Is there any part of you that feels tense, tight, or closed off?

Body-based acceptance starts with being aware of what you're feeling physically without the need to push it away or change it immediately. If you notice areas of discomfort, you can bring gentle attention to them and work through them without being rushed.

From here, you can begin to bring slow movement into the process. Start with gentle stretches or simple movements like rolling your shoulders, stretching your neck, or slowly twisting your torso. Don't force any movements too far; just bring it to a point where you feel slight tension and can tell that the tight muscle is being stretched.

You'll be able to notice where you might be holding tension or where movement feels more restricted. You might also find that certain movements bring up emotions, like a tightness in your chest or a knot in your stomach. Let those sensations pass, and try not to push them away. By allowing them to surface, you give your body permission to process them.

Another important aspect of body-based acceptance is to engage in activities that bring you back into your body in a nurturing way. This might include activities like yoga, meditation, or even dancing; anything that helps you reconnect with the physical self while also inviting in emotional release.

When you try out things like this, please remember to focus on how your body feels and not how your body looks. When you focus on that, you start to create tension in your muscles in the wrong areas to try to make yourself look or feel better in the process. Don't do this. Allow yourself to fully experience the sensations of the movement, whether that's a stretch of muscle, the flow of energy, or the rhythm of your breath.

You can also practice body-based acceptance through touch. Many people find comfort in self-care rituals like massaging their hands or feet or using lotion to nurture their skin. This communicates to your body that it is still worthy of love and attention. You might also explore the power of touch through external sources, like something as simple as being accepting of hugs. It's completely normal to not want anyone to touch you or be in your personal bubble—but if you give a little effort to breaking down that barrier a bit and give in to it, it could be helpful for you.

The act of touch, whether self-directed or shared with others, can show your body that it is safe. Be gentle with yourself as you navigate this process. Discomfort and resistance are expected, and you can work through them. Your body has carried the weight of your pain for so long that releasing it will feel odd and unsettling. Vulnerable, even.

As you begin to embrace what has happened, compassion for yourself will become essential. You are not at war with your past or with the defenses your mind has built to keep you safe. With patience and support, the harsh details will gradually loosen and create space for more positive and healing emotions to take root. The burden you've carried will lighten, allowing peace to emerge—not because the pain never existed but because you have found the strength to acknowledge it and move forward.

Once you've found a way to work through the tension your body is holding, you can look forward to not having to deal with this in the future. Marking a future day of acceptance is a powerful way to set an intention for healing without forcing yourself to be "over" something before you're ready. You've taken time to do exercises that promote your acceptance, and now it's time to make it official.

Choosing a future date allows you to give yourself time and space to grieve, process, and work through current emotions without rushing. The key is to not set the date too soon. If you pick a date only a few weeks away, you might unintentionally create pressure to rush your healing. Instead, choose a timeframe that feels both realistic and challenging, perhaps six months or one year from now. This way, the day becomes a checkpoint rather than a deadline.

Once you've chosen your date, mark it on your calendar, set a reminder in your phone, and clear your schedule that day. Label it something meaningful like *My Acceptance Day* or *My Check-in Point* or even *My New Chapter Begins*. Making it official signals to you that this is an important milestone. As the date approaches, you won't feel a sudden dramatic shift; rather, you will have given yourself the time to do the work of healing without needing immediate resolution.

Leading up to your checkpoint day, allow yourself to reflect on what still lingers. Are there emotions still unresolved? Do you still find yourself lashing out at things or having trigger responses? What parts of your story still feel raw? Use this time to engage in activities that help you process those emotions. Activities like journaling, therapy, meditation, or talking to someone you trust are easy solutions to preparing you mentally for the day.

On the contrary, you might not feel any emotions regarding it. Maybe the work you have done up to this point has been thorough and laid a true foundation for you. Either way, this day will be a day to cherish.

When it finally comes, set aside time for you to acknowledge it fully. Ideally, you might have cleared your calendar or at least half the day to celebrate your progress and be proud of yourself. Do things you love on this day or things you don't typically get to treat yourself to.

Ask yourself, *Have I made peace with what happened? Have I let go of resistance? Am I ready to move forward without carrying this weight any longer?* If the answer is yes, take a symbolic action to honor it. Light a candle, release your reminder object, go to a place that brings you peace, and sit in the stillness to honor your strength.

If, however, you find you have not yet reached full acceptance, *it's okay.* This is not a failure; it just means you need more time. There is no standard timeline for any of this. Realizing you are not ready yet is simply information, an indication that there is still work to be done. Take note of what still feels unsettled.

Is it lingering anger? Unanswered questions? A wound that still feels fresh and hard to talk about? If you realize you need more time, set a new check-in date for yourself and make note of what worked and what didn't for the first one. Acceptance does not happen on command, and realizing you might not be there yet or giving yourself more time and more grace is part of the process.

If you find that you haven't made much progress with the previous remedies, utilizing support groups can be helpful. Sharing your experience with others who have walked similar paths can provide validation, comfort, and connection. It's easy to think that nobody understands what you're going through, so hearing similar experiences from others can be eye-opening. Support groups offer a sense of community, reminding you that you are not alone. These groups form special bonds and offer a space where empathy and healing are intertwined, making the process feel less isolating.

Finding the courage to join a support group or seek a peer mentor can feel humiliating. A sense of vulnerability comes with opening up to others and admitting you need extra help, that healing by yourself isn't working. It's a punch to the ego. It's normal to worry about judgment, about whether others will understand, or even about feeling exposed to a group of people you don't know. It's important to remind yourself that vulnerability is the bridge to connection and that you will be met with kindness in these spaces because everyone involved is just like you—trying to heal from similar experiences.

Finding the right group or mentor begins with exploration. You'll have a ton of options. Research local options first or, if you prefer privacy, search for online options like social media groups or pages. Many communities offer low-cost support groups and online forums dedicated to specific types of trauma.

Look for groups where the facilitator or mentor is trained, where confidentiality is respected, and where the focus is on mutual support rather than on "fixing" one another. This space should allow for open expression without pressure to join.

When you attend your first meeting or connect with your peer mentor, approach with an open heart and mind. You'll have feelings of uncertainty; let them flow and keep moving forward. You shouldn't be required to speak until you're ready—just being involved and listening to others can be powerful.

There is a lot of comfort in hearing others share their feelings, struggles, and experiences just like yours. This sense of solidarity is relieving and is one of the best things a support group offers.

There will be moments when you feel strong and moments when you feel weak or vulnerable, and that's perfectly normal. Being part of a support group allows you to witness the ups and downs of a "normal" journey. Your role in the group or relationship with a mentor is just as important as the group's role in your healing. By sharing your experience with people around you, you provide them with validation and understanding. In turn, the act of helping others can reinforce your healing because it allows you to see your own growth and reflect on how far you've come.

Don't underestimate the power of your presence. Sometimes, just being there, listening, and sharing your story can help both you and other participants feel seen.

In due time, your day of acceptance will arrive, and you will feel it in your bones. It will be instinctive. The day you set will serve as your marker for how far you've come and for new beginnings to start. Through acceptance, you learn to embrace this deeper version of yourself. You are still you, just evolving. Change is not the enemy; it's a natural part of life. It's a hurdle. The way you respond to your own experiences now will not be the way you always respond to them in the future. Growth is inevitable. Don't worry.

Chapter 4

Honesty Over Silence

Releasing the Weight of Shame

When life turns upside down, honesty—especially with yourself—can be one of the most daunting challenges. The truth can feel like an immovable force, standing in the way of the fragile stability you're so desperately trying to hold on to. In the face of pain, the instinct to turn away or to shield yourself from the rawness of reality is automatic. We convince ourselves that if we don't acknowledge something, then maybe it won't hurt so much. Yes, it's there and it's making eyes at you, asking for your attention, but as long as we keep walking the other way, it won't hurt us.

Avoidance, no matter how well-intentioned, has a way of turning into self-deception. The more we cling to false truth and ignore reality, the heavier things become. Emotions, even positive ones, become dulled, and you aren't able to enjoy things as you should.

Shame is a heavy burden we carry after trauma. Unlike guilt, which is linked with regret for a specific action, shame seeps deeper, causing us to think the pain we carry is a reflection of who we are. Shame tells us in a whisper that we are broken, we caused this, this is our fault, something is wrong with us, and that if people could truly see who we are, they would reject us.

This causes us to continue our journey in silence, fed by the fear that our suffering and pain are too much, too messy, too complicated, and too overwhelming for anyone else to deal with.

You're going to have to navigate how to let go of your ego as you're preparing to embrace honesty. Your ego acts as a barrier, convincing you that admitting that certain experiences or emotions are hard for you is a sign of weakness or failure. It tells you that you should have been smarter, stronger, or more aware to prevent painful situations from happening in the first place. This belief can make honesty feel embarrassing, as if revealing your truth exposes your flaws. However, the reality is that life is unpredictable, and no amount of intelligence or strength can completely shield you from harm, pain, mistakes, or trauma.

The ego clings to your identity and to the idea that being a competent and resilient person who is always in control is the only way to be. It makes certain truths feel like a threat. You might think, *How could I let that happen to me?* Or *I'm not the kind of person who goes through things like this.* These thoughts create shame, making it harder to speak openly. Releasing the need to uphold a perfect image allows you to speak with authenticity rather than self-protection.

When you release the high standards that you're holding yourself to and drop your ego, you allow yourself to tell your truth without fear, shame, or the need for validation. You remove the pressure to appear perfect and replace it with the freedom to be yourself. The second you stop seeing your truth as something that diminishes you and start seeing it as something that strengthens you and can mold you into a better human being, the sooner the fear of embarrassment or being seen as *less-than* will subside. What remains is a deep sense of liberation, self-acceptance, and the realization that speaking your truth is not an act of weakness but one of the greatest acts of strength.

When you're preparing to face the raw reality of things, create a "lie vs. truth" chart. This can be a good tool to use when you need to practice self-awareness. This chart serves as a tangible way to distinguish the falsehoods you might tell yourself from the realities that can lead to healing. This is similar to the truth statements discussed in the previous chapter, but they can be more specifically geared toward your situation and the exact events that occurred.

By visually mapping out the contrast between the two perspectives, you can begin to pick apart and change the deceptive narratives that keep you stuck in pain and avoidance. Doing this encourages you to look deep within yourself to see how much denial has influenced your perception of the past. Writing things out forces you to make a choice: continue believing the falsehood, or start embracing the reality.

This exercise also provides clarity and validation. Lies tend to be vague or emotionally charged, while truth is often more grounded and empowering. When people see their truths written out in front of them, they gain a clearer perspective on their experiences.

Here's an example of something you could write: let's say the traumatic event in question is a car crash. The lie in this event might be something like, *I should have had faster reflexes and gained control of the car better*, which leans toward the idea that you were wrong and it's all your fault. This is the kind of thinking that keeps people silent. On the other hand, the truth in that statement could look like, *I was going the speed limit and paying attention, then hydroplaned, which was completely out of my control, and I didn't have the capacity to correct anything before it happened*. Do you see what we're going for here? I want you to discuss what happened with yourself in a way that is matter-of-fact and doesn't blame and shame you.

To untangle shame, we must first see it for what it is: a distortion of the truth, not a measure of our worth. Shame thrives in secrecy but loses its grip when met with understanding and compassion. Being seen in your truth opens the door to connection, and from that space of connection, we can begin to rewrite the false narratives that we are carrying around with us.

Close your eyes and picture a moment when you are fully honest about your trauma, either in your own mind or with someone you trust. Imagine everything goes well. The person listening holds your hand and responds with warmth and understanding. Imagine they make no judgment, only giving support instead. Imagine feeling lighter as the weight of holding in this truth lifts from your shoulders. Your words, once trapped inside, now exist outside of you. Imagine they bring you no harm, only clarity. How does that feel?

Now, shift your focus to the worst-case scenario. Imagine the listener reacts with discomfort, disbelief, and even dismissal. Imagine they change the subject quickly or begin invalidating your experience. Or worse, imagine they respond with total silence and look at you like something is wrong with you. Imagine their reaction feels heavier than the trauma you just shared. Imagine yourself feeling exposed and vulnerable and regretting the act of sharing. How does that feel?

Now, bring your attention back to yourself. The reality is that the reaction you're most likely to get when sharing your truth is somewhere between those two scenarios. No matter what the reaction is, the truth does not change, and the importance of it does not change either. Whether the worst- or best-case scenario plays out, being honest is a choice you make for your own well-being, not for the approval of others.

Imagine standing in front of a mirror and saying your truth out loud, just to yourself. Watch as the words take shape; notice how they feel in your body. The truth exists whether or not it is met with understanding.

If you visualize this moment of self-honesty, you'll realize that the most important response to your truth is your own.

Imagine that after sharing your truth, the initial discomfort gives way to relief. The fear of speaking up gradually fades, to be replaced by strength and empowerment. Now that you've shared it, you no longer have to carry the burden alone. Perhaps the person you confide in responds with kindness, or maybe they relate to your experience and you end up having a deeper connection. Even if they don't fully understand, their presence reminds you that you don't have to go through this all by yourself.

Preparing to embrace this honesty begins within you. It's the first hurdle you have to work through once you realize what has happened. Something that can help with that is sensory deprivation. Sensory deprivation is practiced through mediums like float therapy or meditation in a dark, silent space. It's a way to remove all distractions so the only thing left to do is look within.

Our world is filled with so much noise and external stimulation, which makes it easy to avoid self-reflection. By stripping away these outside influences, sensory deprivation leaves you alone with your thoughts and emotions, creating space for you to confront those feelings. Scary, right? But necessary.

Acknowledging the truths within yourself in a safe space makes it easier to share them with others. At first, putting yourself in a sensory deprivation situation can be unsettling. It lets unsettled emotions and memories resurface. However, letting these feelings emerge in a calm and controlled environment allows you to process them without judgment or witnesses.

Beyond helping you with self-reflection, sensory deprivation promotes relaxation and reduces your stress levels, making it easier to process difficult emotions. When your body reaches a state of deep relaxation, the brain shifts from high-frequency activity linked to stress to a much slower, more meditative state. In this state, pulling out subconscious thoughts and emotions becomes a lot easier and can be done without resistance and fear. Clarity about certain events might come naturally, and insights about your past or present struggles can emerge on their own without you trying to resolve them.

Sensory deprivation is also good for emotional regulation. Without background noise and distractions, you can tune into everything in your mind. You might begin to recognize thought patterns and emotional triggers, and you can pick apart the negative stories you tell yourself.

With this awareness, you can gain more control over your reactions and responses. This is particularly useful when preparing to be honest about difficult experiences. Instead of reacting impulsively out of fear or defensiveness, you can approach conversations with a sense of calm and self-assurance.

When you spend time alone in a distraction-free environment, you learn to rely on your own internal guidance rather than seeking validation from people around you. You become more secure and less afraid of rejection or judgment because you have already accepted your own truth internally.

We're often told honesty is the best policy, yet when conversations shift toward pain, trauma, grief, or loss, an uncomfortable elephant steps into the room. This is why we instinctively pull away and can be unsure of what to say or how to react to someone else's suffering. This unspoken fear lingers that if we acknowledge the pain, we will be giving it more power, or that putting words to hardship will somehow make it heavier and worse. So, we learn to dilute our own truth. Downplaying struggles becomes second nature, not only to protect others from discomfort but also to shield ourselves from the full weight of our own experiences.

Exposure therapy is a psychological technique that you can use to help yourself confront your own fears and anxieties in a controlled and gradual manner. Although its often used for the purpose of working through phobias or things like PTSD, it can also be a valuable tool for preparing to speak your truth, especially when that truth is tied to trauma or emotional wounds. The idea of exposure therapy provides a structured and nonconfrontational way to face these fears step-by-step, which can make being honest and having those harsh conversations feel more manageable.

The key idea of exposure therapy is gradual desensitization. It's when you slowly increase exposure to a feared or out-of-the-ordinary situation until it no longer causes you distress and anxiety. When applied to speaking the truth, this might begin with small, low-risk acts of honesty like speaking the truth out loud in a public setting to people who don't know you and don't care or in an anonymous setting like a chat room or online group.

For example, you could tell the cashier at the grocery store about something stressful that happened at work. Something harmless, of course, and definitely don't waste anyone's time by standing there and holding up the line to tell them about something that happened in one of your meetings. You can, however, tell them just a minor and random frustrating detail about your day. They might look at you funny, like "Did I ask?" You might get stared at, or you might even get that uncomfortable laugh we tend to give people who can't read a room.

The point is to share something uncomfortable and be able to brace yourself for that odd reaction. You aren't doing anything illegal or burdening anyone; you're just exposing yourself a bit more than you're used to. This allows you to see an off-putting reaction and learn to process it.

When you repeatedly avoid difficult conversations, your brain can begin to associate honesty with danger. This avoidance reinforces your fear without you even knowing it. Exposure therapy disrupts this cycle by proving through direct experience that honesty doesn't always lead to disaster—sometimes you'll get just an uncomfortable reaction. Over time, the brain can get used to this and can unlearn the fear it's adopted in speaking the truth. You can reteach it to understand that the truth can be safe, cathartic, and even empowering.

Another major benefit of exposure therapy is that it gets you into the habit of better regulating your emotions. By gradually facing odd or difficult emotions in a controlled way, you become less likely to shut down, disassociate, or become overwhelmed. This makes you less fearful of losing control of the conversation. Learning to tolerate discomfort in small doses strengthens your emotional resilience and makes it easier for you to stay present and composed.

Softening the edges of our story or presenting it in a more digestible way is a form of keeping control. Pretending that things are fine can sometimes feel easier than facing the truth head-on. But reshaping pain to make it more palatable chips away at authenticity. The more you suppress your emotions or alter your story, the further you'll find yourself drifting from not only others but also from yourself. The growing distance will leave you feeling isolated, unseen, unheard, and disconnected.

To start to overcome anxiety about opening up, ask yourself, *In ten years, will I regret staying silent?* or, *How will I feel a decade from now if I choose honesty today?* Doing this shifts your focus from short-term fear to long-term consequences. Visualize how your future self will look back on your choices, and you might be able to gain some clarity on whether or not the honesty is worth the temporary discomfort.

In a decade, will you wish you had been more honest with people? Will you regret not expressing your true emotions or needs? Maybe you'll have stronger bonds with people because you spoke up. You don't think about it every day. It doesn't stress you out or give you anxiety anymore because you've worked through it. So, even though this feels like a tough task right now, there will be bigger, better, more important things in your life in ten years, and holding on to this burden for that long will only weigh you down. Instead of making decisions based on temporary fear, make them based on the idea of long-term fulfillment.

The longer you uphold a false narrative, the more exhausting it becomes. Every interaction requires careful navigation of what you reveal, what you conceal, and what version of the story is best or easiest. Anxiety, stress, and even physical symptoms like headaches, fatigue, or sleep loss, and even digestive issues, can manifest when your mind and body are at war with the truth.

The last concept I want to share with you is something called tapping. Or, in more complex terms, emotional freedom technique (EFT). Tapping is a mind-to-body practice designed to reduce stress, release emotional blockages, and replace negative thought patterns. It combines elements of acupressure and cognitive therapy by using gentle tapping techniques on specific meridian points of the body.

When you focus on a specific issue or emotion while tapping, it can help regulate your nervous system and break down emotional patterns associated with past trauma. It promotes a sense of calmness and clarity. It's particularly effective for those struggling to express their truth, and it can help alleviate fear and anxiety.

To begin a tapping session, find a quiet and comfortable space where you can focus without distractions. Start by identifying a specific issue or fear you want to address. It could be fear of speaking the truth and opening up about what you're going through, anxiety about how others will react, or maybe it's something about a deeper emotional wound related to your experiences. Once you have identified your focus, rate your discomfort on a scale from zero to ten. This can help you measure your progress as you go through the process.

The tapping session involves gently tapping on a series of meridian points on the body, usually with two or three fingers. The primary points used in ETF are the side of the hand (karate chop point), the eyebrow, the side of the eye, under the eye, under the nose, on the chin, on the collarbone, under the arm, and on the top of the head. These specific points correspond to energy pathways in the body.

Begin tapping on the side of your hand while stating a setup phrase that acknowledges your current struggle while also offering self-acceptance. For example, you might say, "Though I am afraid to speak my truth, I completely accept myself as I am right now." Repeat the phrase three or four times while continuing to tap on the side of your hand. This sets the foundation for the tapping sequence by acknowledging the issue.

Next, move through the different tapping points while stating reminders of your emotion or fear. Start at the eyebrow and say something like, "I'm afraid of being judged." Move to the side of your eye and say something like, "I worry about what people will think." Under the eye, continue with, "It's hard for me to be honest." Under the nose, you can say, "What if speaking my truth makes things worse?" At the collarbone: "This fear is weighing on me." Then, under the arm: "I feel stuck in this pattern." Finally, at the top of your head: "I don't know how to move forward."

The narrative you use when tapping can be anything you're feeling. The idea is to talk yourself through your emotions and why you feel them. After completing one round of tapping, take a deep breath and check in with yourself. Rate your level of distress again on a scale from zero to ten. If the intensity has decreased but the feeling is still there, continue tapping for another round, adjusting the language slightly to reflect any shifts in your feelings. If your emotions begin to change, you can start incorporating positive affirmations into your tapping, such as, "Maybe I can find the courage to do this" or, "I believe in myself."

Tapping is also an effective way to break free from limiting beliefs. Many fears about speaking the truth stem from deep-seated beliefs formed in childhood or through past experiences. When you choose to address these beliefs directly through tapping, you can begin to replace them with more empowering narratives. For instance, someone who was taught that expressing emotions only leads to rejection might be able to shift their mindset by tapping with a phrase like, "My truth is valuable, and I deserve to be heard."

Love and connection lose their depth when built on a version of you that isn't entirely real. Those around you might care for you deeply and sincerely, but if they only see what you allow them to, how can their love ever feel genuine? True belonging cannot exist without authenticity. Only by allowing yourself to be seen with your flaws and your pain can you experience the kind of connection that is both real and lasting. The risk of honesty might feel daunting, but the alternative is a life spent wondering if anyone truly knows you at all.

Whether or not you feel ready to share your truth, it's important to carefully consider who you choose to open up to. Not everyone deserves access to your vulnerability, and that's perfectly okay. Being honest about your experience is an intimate act, and it requires the right kind of space and support. Some people in your life will be able to offer empathy and understanding, providing the support you need. Others, however, might not have the capacity to do so, and their responses might not align with what you need in that moment. Recognizing this distinction helps prevent disappointment and helps you protect yourself during such a delicate moment.

Think about who in your life has shown the ability to listen to you without judgment. These are the people who will not rush to fix or minimize your pain but will instead offer a safe and open ear. They allow you to express yourself without pushing for solutions or trying to reshape your reality. The people you choose should make you feel seen and heard, not like you need to defend your truth, argue why you hadn't told them yet, or justify your feelings. They don't just listen; they witness your experience, accepting it as valid, no matter how messy or difficult it might be.

Determining who to share your story with often involves tuning in to your own intuition. Think about the people who have shown up for you in the past, not just in good times but when things were difficult. Who has demonstrated patience and a willingness to hear you out, even when they knew they didn't have all the answers? These are the individuals you need to look for because they are the ones you can turn to first. If nobody comes to mind immediately, just take some time to reflect and consider. This conversation will be important, and it deserves careful thought.

While you might feel a mix of fear and anticipation when it comes time to speak, remember that you are in full control of where, when, and how quickly you share everything. If you choose to speak to someone and their reaction is dismissive or hurtful, it's crucial that you don't internalize their response. Their inability to fully grasp your experience doesn't diminish what you've gone through. Your truth remains unchanged, regardless of how it is received, and you know that. In those moments, remind yourself that their reaction is more about them than it is about you.

Having this conversation with the right person can be incredibly healing, but it's also important to protect yourself from potential harm. If someone's response is not supportive or validating, it's okay to set boundaries and withdraw from the conversation. You don't need to continue sharing if it's causing you more pain. There will be others who can offer you support, and in time, you'll find those who will help you carry the weight of your experience just by being present with you.

When getting ready for that conversation, set the tone and establish an environment where both you and the other person can approach the discussion with openness and understanding. Before diving into all the details, give them a heads-up that you need to talk about something difficult and personal with them. Let them know that what you say might be hard for them to hear. Acknowledging up front that the conversation might be emotional for both of you can help ease anxiety. It's also an important opportunity to let them know their support means a lot to you and that you're trusting them with something that might bring up strong feelings. Setting the tone allows everyone to mentally prepare.

When you open up, the person you're speaking to might have their own emotional reaction. They might feel anxiety, anger, fear, sadness, or even guilt about what you've gone through. It's not uncommon for them to cry or need a moment to process what they're hearing. This is a natural response when someone cares a lot about you and is moved by your pain. These deep emotional responses are a reflection of their strong connection to you. If they do become emotional, don't feel like you need to rush to comfort them or change the subject. Allow them the time to process, just as you need time to share. Reassure them that it's okay for both of you to feel strongly during this conversation.

Once you've had the conversation and the initial emotions have settled, have a plan for what comes next. Being vulnerable and opening up about something so personal is draining, and it's normal to feel like you don't have the energy to continue having the same conversation with multiple people.

The person you're speaking with can play an essential role in helping you navigate that. After they've heard your story and processed their own emotions, you can ask them to help you share your experience with others if needed. This can take the burden off you, especially when you don't have the capacity to keep repeating everything. They can help relay information about what is going on to other friends or family members in a way that respects your boundaries and ensures that you don't have to live it over and over.

Having someone else involved in sharing your story can also provide a sense of validation and support. When others are made aware of your experience, it not only helps to relieve some of the emotional labor of constant retelling but also opens up a network of people who can offer their support in different ways. You don't have to bear the weight of your truth alone; with the right people in your life, the act of sharing becomes less isolating. This support system can help you heal without overburdening yourself emotionally. It's important to allow yourself to rest, knowing that others can carry part of the load with you. That's the beauty of having people so close to you in your life, after all.

Shame cannot survive in the light. The more we speak, the less power it holds. Naming our experiences without dressing them up or making them more digestible for others is an act of reclamation. It is saying blatantly, *This happened. This is real. I am still here.* Forgiveness can be a part of the process too—not necessarily for others but for yourself. For the ways you coped. For the things you didn't know then that you do know now. For the weight you've carried for far too long.

When you allow yourself to be truly seen, you realize that you are not as alone as you once believed. There is always going to be someone else who understands. Beyond that, the relationships that you cultivate (the ones that you don't feel the need to edit yourself for) become stronger, deeper, and more authentic. In those spaces, you are not just tolerated; you are embraced.

Some days you might feel ready to stand in your truth—confident and clear about expressing yourself. Other days, silence might feel like the safer option due to it providing a sense of comfort and protection. Both are valid parts of the journey. It's important to remember this: you do not owe anyone your silence. You do not have to shrink yourself or keep quiet to make others comfortable. The people who truly care about you will never ask you to. They will embrace you just as you are, honoring your need for both speaking up and resting in quiet. And if someone is ever asking you to keep quiet, to not tell anybody, or to act like it didn't happen, odds are that the particular person is either guilty of something, knows they did something wrong, or they're simply okay with your suffering and think that hiding is more important. Don't ever listen to them.

Chapter 5

Rediscovering Health

A Journey of Physical and Mental Well-Being

In recent years, self-care has become a popular and essential practice for maintaining a healthy mind and body. Although it was once considered a luxury or even an act of selfishness, it's now widely recognized as a normal part of our overall well-being. The stigma around self-care has faded, and we've come to understand that prioritizing our own needs is not only healthy but also necessary. Self-care goes beyond the occasional indulgence like getting your nails done, going to the spa, or taking a mental health day. When we nurture our body, mind, and spirit, we provide ourselves with the resources we need to heal.

Healing from trauma requires understanding the deep connection between the body and mind. Trauma affects not only our emotional or mental state, unfortunately. It often manifests physically in ways that can be persistent and disruptive. One common physical symptom of emotional distress is chronic pain, especially for those who might have endured long-term trauma. The body tends to store stress in certain areas, such as the neck, shoulders, and back, which can lead to a lot of extra tension and tightness. Over time, this can escalate into conditions like chronic migraines, back pain, or even fibromyalgia, where widespread pain becomes a constant companion. It can feel as if the body itself is holding onto the emotional weight, making relief seem out of reach, no matter how much rest or treatment is sought.

Trauma can even have effects on your digestive system, which is often referred to as your "second brain." Your gut is incredibly sensitive to emotional stress, and when you experience trauma, you might find yourself dealing with digestive issues like bloating, indigestion, or irregular bowel movements. These issues often get worse during times of anxiety or emotional stress. You might also notice significant shifts in your appetite, either overeating as a form of self-soothing or losing interest in food altogether. The physical effects of trauma are wide-ranging and can really have an impact on how our body functions daily.

The tension that trauma creates becomes embedded in our muscles, posture, and overall physical presence. This is why sometimes you might feel disconnected or out of sync with yourself. This physical disconnection can make it difficult to feel safe or grounded, especially when emotional triggers arise. Reestablishing a sense of embodiment, one where you feel present and at home again in your own body, becomes a vital part of the healing journey.

One of the most effective ways to release that built-up tension is through gentle movement. Activities like stretching, yoga, or even taking a short walk can help the body gradually unwind and restore a better sense of ease. These simple movements create an opportunity to reconnect with your body and cultivate a feeling of comfort within it. As you engage in these practices, it's important to pay attention to your body's signals and approach them with compassion and patience. Gentle movement can also help break through emotional blockages that have been stored physically, allowing feelings or memories that might have been suppressed to surface.

Yoga, in particular, can be especially beneficial for trauma recovery because it combines physical movement with breathwork. Focusing gently on your body and your breath helps you relax, ease anxiety, and let go of built-up tension. The slow, deliberate movements in yoga create space for emotional release, which offers a way for you to process your feelings in a nonverbal way. In the same way, regular stretching can ease physical discomfort, improve flexibility and circulation, and give your body a chance to loosen up and recover from stress. Remember to start at a pace that feels comfortable and within your body's limits.

In a similar spirit of reconnecting with the body and building resilience, something a little out of the box that you can do is something called cold plunging. Cold plunging has gained popularity as a tool for supporting both physical and mental well-being. I know . . . you're probably thinking you're going to skip this. Cold plunging can (and does) seem a little outlandish to the average person.

If you're an adrenaline junkie like me, or you're looking to feel like you have control over your body again, it might be worth a shot. Immersing your body in freezing water for short periods triggers a natural fight-or-flight response. This sounds counter-intuitive when you are trying to heal and not be in fight-or-flight 24/7, but this time it's in a controlled environment and you can expect it. This leads to the release of endorphins, which helps you improve your mood and reduce stress. The surge of chemicals in your body brings a sense of euphoria, which is typically followed by a burst of energy and positivity.

In the same way we tend to yearn for the summer in the winter and vice-versa, when you cold plunge, you can almost immediately expect to be more grateful and appreciative of warmth and steadiness once it's complete. It's easier to find comfort and a sense of well-being when you aren't in a freezing cold body of water anymore.

With regular practice, cold plunging can train your body and mind to adapt more effectively to stress, allowing you to move through daily challenges and triggers with much greater ease. Completing a cold plunge also serves as a powerful reminder of your own inner strength. It reinforces the idea that you can face discomfort head-on and come out stronger, which builds confidence. You'll find you feel inspired to meet other challenges with the same courage it takes to complete a cold plunge.

Beyond the immediate mood-boosting effects, cold plunging can enhance mental clarity and focus. It immediately snaps you into the present and makes you alert and hyperaware of your surroundings. When you immerse yourself in the freezing water, your body increases circulation, which sends oxygen-rich blood to your brain, sharpening your cognitive function. Many people who practice cold plunging report feeling more alert and clearheaded afterward, making it a valuable tool for those who need to sharpen their mental focus. The experience forces you to stay present in the moment and focus on your breath, which is an incredible tool overall in the long run.

The key to these practices is consistency and learning to listen to your body's needs. It might feel unfamiliar at first, especially if you're used to pushing through discomfort or ignoring your body's signals. That's okay. Healing takes time and intention. As you continue to engage in restorative activities over time, you'll feel a big shift in ownership. This shift won't be in just how your body feels physically but also in how you perceive yourself and your emotions. You might find yourself feeling more in tune with your inner world and better able to recognize what you need in those fleeting moments of stress or discomfort. As long as you keep practicing patience and perseverance, you will gradually begin to reclaim your body and restore the balance and harmony between your mind and physical self.

In the healing process, mental health often needs to come before physical health. That's not to say your body and physical health don't matter or are not important, because they are. However, when we are emotionally drained and overwhelmed, it's incredibly difficult to take care of our physical health in a positive and effective way. Even the simplest habits like eating well, staying hydrated, and getting enough rest can feel out of reach when your mind is consumed by distress. Emotional well-being provides a strong foundation for improving your physical well-being. When you feel emotionally supported and regulated, it's easier to make choices to care for your physical self as well. By tending to your inner world, you create the conditions for your whole self to begin flourishing.

Approach your journey toward health with love and acceptance. Do not allow societal pressures or unrealistic expectations to define your path. Start from a place of compassion, not comparison. Starting from a place of compassion makes the pursuit of health a lot more sustainable and meaningful. Instead of focusing on outward appearances, prioritize honoring your body and mind just as they are. Focusing on health for the right reasons—because you want to *feel* better rather than because you feel obligated to meet a certain standard—lead to a much simpler and safer, long-lasting experience.

It's also worth recognizing that emotional health and physical health are connected in ways that we often don't even fully realize until something feels off. You might find yourself wanting to make positive changes like eating better or getting more exercise, yet you might feel heavy resistance that's hard to explain. That resistance is emotional, and it can quietly drain both your energy and motivation. For many people, this is where depression can take shape.

It's difficult when you know you need to get better or do better but you just can't seem to get yourself to move. Depression slips in as dull fatigue or a sense of disconnection, even a noticeable loss of interest in things you once enjoyed. When your inner world feels so weighed down, caring for your physical self can be incredibly difficult. The mental and emotional weight can be overwhelming, making even the simplest tasks feel like monumental efforts.

Sometimes, healing can be an incredibly lonely process, especially when you start to outgrow the people, patterns, and places that once made you feel safe. When you begin to turn inward, it means you have to step back from external noise. The constant distractions, favors, relationships built around survival, or habits that help to keep you numb, they all have to go away. You might catch yourself missing the chaos, craving connection, or even wondering if the loneliness means you're doing something wrong. You're not. It doesn't. It means you're starting to listen to yourself again.

There's a sting that comes with realizing that not everyone will understand or be there for your healing. Some people simply might not see you as a benefit to them anymore and might turn away when you start setting those boundaries. Some people are comfortable with the version of you that carried their pain, dimmed your light, or avoided your truth. When you start protecting your peace, it can make others uncomfortable and guilty, especially those who benefited from your self-neglect. It's natural to wonder if your growth is worth the distance it creates. Still, sometimes healing means stepping back first, so real connection has a chance to form again.

Loneliness isn't a punishment, though it can feel like it. When you strip away those distractions and false safeties, you start to meet yourself in a more honest and sincere way. You learn what your own voice sounds like when no one else is influencing it. You notice the small details again, things like the way your energy shifts, the moments that make you feel peaceful, and the activities that fill you up instead of draining you. You can be your own source of comfort; I promise you that.

Solitude is not the same as isolation. Isolation disconnects you from life; solitude reconnects you to it. It gives you time to recalibrate and rediscover what feels right to your body and spirit. It's during those quiet stretches that you can find new clarity and realize what you want to bring back into your life and what you no longer have the space for. Sometimes, the loneliness itself becomes the teacher and shows you what parts of yourself have been neglected for far too long.

There is also grief in healing. Grief about who you used to be, of relationships that no longer align, or of dreams that no longer fit. It's natural to feel lost when the old ways have stopped working but the new ones don't work yet or haven't formed yet. That in-between space can feel endless and depressing. Just try to remember that loneliness often means you're just in between two different versions of yourself—like you're shedding an identity that was built around pain and waiting to grow into one that is built around peace.

The beauty of this season is that it won't last forever. As you continue to nurture yourself, your energy will begin to attract people and experiences that match where you're going instead of where you've been. The loneliness will soften into peace. You'll learn how to enjoy your own company and how to feel safe in your own presence again. What once felt like emptiness will now feel like freedom.

Healing asks you to be brave enough to sit in that quiet and let the stillness do its work. The loneliness you feel isn't a void; it's a clearing. It's making space for new energy, new people, and a new version of yourself. It's important to try to remember these things when you're in this stage. Being mindful of things like this can help you to avoid slipping into that depressing state of mind.

During this part of the process, it's easy to confuse progress with peace. You might expect that once you start healing, you'll immediately feel lighter, but the truth is, healing often stirs things up before it settles them down. The quiet can bring emotions to the surface that you've avoided for years, and that can feel heavy. These are the moments when self-awareness really matters. When you recognize that discomfort is part of growth, it's easier to stay steady instead of feeling defeated.

If depression takes hold, it can throw off your body's natural rhythms, including sleep patterns. Many people struggling with depression experience burnout and restlessness. They can have difficulty falling asleep and might wake up frequently throughout the night. When the body and mind can't rest properly, it creates a vicious cycle. Poor sleep quality leads to increased stress, and the lack of truly restorative sleep makes it even harder to heal from that emotional and physical fatigue that you're struggling with. Without enough deep, restful sleep, the body can't repair itself and restore the energy it needs to navigate daily life.

Sleep is when the body repairs tissues, replenishes your energy, and regulates your emotions. During deep sleep, the brain processes and consolidates memories, which helps you to manage and process your emotions. This is why a healthy sleep routine plays such a crucial role in supporting both your physical and mental well-being. When you build consistent sleep habits, you give your body the chance to recover from the exhaustion that comes with stress, depression, or burnout. You also wake up with more energy to handle each day with strength and steadiness.

Rest is one of the most misunderstood parts of healing. If you've lived in survival mode for a long period of time, slowing down and turning off your body and mind doesn't feel peaceful; it feels unsafe. When your body has become so used to constant vigilance, stillness can trigger discomfort and even guilt. You might sit down to relax, then suddenly you feel uneasy or like you *should* be doing something. This is your nervous system still learning to adjust after years of being on alert.

Learning to rest again seems so simple, but it's really an act of strength and perseverance. It means teaching your body that safety doesn't require movement or productivity. True rest involves allowing yourself to exist without performing, fixing, or proving anything. It's about giving yourself permission to pause, not because you've *earned it* but because you *need it.* You have to have it, even.

Rest doesn't always mean sleep. Sometimes it's just sitting in silence for a few minutes, stepping outside to breathe fresh air, or lying down in the middle of the day without explanation or guilt. Rest is also emotional, pulling back from overstimulation and releasing those expectations. It involves you giving yourself permission to recharge for a moment without having to over-explain or justify it. Many people mistake rest for weakness, but in reality, it takes some serious self-awareness and strength to stop doing and start being.

For trauma survivors especially, rest can be the most powerful self-care practice of all. Being able to relax without fear or stress tells your nervous system that it's safe to finally let go. Over time, it helps your body learn what calm really feels like, shifting your view of stillness from something unsafe to something restorative.

If resting feels impossible at first, try easing into it with intentional stillness. This is something I personally like to do. I'll lie down, close my eyes, and freeze my whole body. Then I count down from one hundred and tell myself I'm not allowed to move a single muscle until I reach zero. If I accidentally twitch or shift even a little, I start over at one hundred and begin again.

When I first started doing this, I could barely make it to eighty without moving. Sometimes it took a dozen tries just to get all the way down to zero without slipping up. Now that I've practiced it consistently, I can usually make it to zero without any trouble. Over time, your body starts to settle more quickly, and you'll find it easier to truly rest, and even fall asleep, because you've trained yourself to be still long enough to recharge.

With more energy and clarity, it becomes easier to begin building a daily routine, even after experiencing trauma that makes a routine so far out of reach. While the idea of creating structure might feel overwhelming at first, it's a meaningful step toward healing and stability. Start by getting clear on what you want to achieve, even if it's something small. This might include carving out time for rest, beginning some full-body stretching, or even just scheduling ten or fifteen minutes a day when you can check in with yourself and your emotions.

Something really helpful that you can do is create a calming nighttime routine. Creating a calming nighttime routine is a powerful way to support both your physical and emotional healing. In today's fast-paced and overstimulating world, it's important to give your body crystal clear signals that it's now time to rest. Reducing your screen time at least an hour before bed can be especially helpfully as the blue light from phones, tablets, televisions, and computers can interfere with your body's natural melatonin production. Instead of scrolling, try engaging in soothing activities like reading a book, taking a warm bath, or journaling.

Create a peaceful sleep environment for yourself that will also promote your rest. Decluttering your bedroom, dimming the lights, and removing loud or disruptive noises helps to encourage your relaxation. Many people also find that white or brown noise is helpful in making background noises that might otherwise disrupt your sleep to be masked or go unnoticed. White noise covers a range of frequencies consistent with a hum, while brown noise has a deeper, softer tone that you might find more comforting.

These steady sounds can soothe the nervous system and reduce sensitivity to external noise, making it easier to fall asleep and stay asleep. I personally like to find a video I can play on my TV that plays brown noise and has a black screen. You can find plenty of these types of videos online with thousands of background sounds and lengths that don't turn off too soon, either.

Once you get used to getting a full night's rest, you won't be so groggy and out of tune all the time, and you'll find it a lot easier to create routines for yourself. Introducing a bit of structure to your day will give you the sense of stability you need without the expectations of having everything done at once.

When you awaken each morning, take a moment to do some deep breathing and light stretching to wake your body and mind up. Avoid immediately doomscrolling on your phone. Look out your window and see what the weather is like, think about your day ahead, and pick three things you'd like to get done. Don't give yourself any time frames or deadlines on these items; just make it a goal to have them done by the end of the day. This way, if you have a few lazy hours where you feel out of touch and unmotivated, you haven't already failed the assignment. The goal is to create habits that feel nurturing and sustainable, not overwhelming.

Give yourself permission to be flexible with these three items. If you don't complete them all every single day, be gracious with yourself. Instead of paying attention to how quickly you might have failed to complete these tasks, pay attention to how quickly you bounce back. Failing to complete one task is not permission to throw away the whole day and not try to complete the other two things. Imagine you're pouring coffee into a mug and you spill a little. Well, you might as well just pour the entire pot of coffee onto the floor, right? Of course not. Clean up the tiny bit you spilled and continue pouring the coffee you want into your mug and carry on with your day.

An easy task that can be first on your list is a guided meditation. Guided meditation is a gentle and powerful tool that supports your emotional healing. At its core, meditation encourages mindfulness, which means observing your own thoughts, emotions, and physical sensations. Meditation helps separate you from your emotional experiences, giving you room to process and release the emotional weight that often follows trauma. You do not necessarily need to sit in silence for extended periods to benefit, either. Doing just a quick ten-minute guided meditation each day can help you cross something off your list without causing disruption to your schedule, and it can even become something you look forward to.

I personally like to find my guided meditations online or with an app on my phone. All you need to do is find a quiet place, sit or lie down in a comfortable position, and press *play*. A guide will walk you through the entire meditation, and that ten minutes will be over before you even realize it. You might even start with ten-minute meditations and find that you enjoy them so much that you increase to thirty minutes or even an hour-long session.

Just as mindfulness strengthens your emotional foundation, nutrition provides the physical support that your body needs to heal. The food you eat does more than just fuel your body; it has a direct impact on your mood and energy levels. During the healing process, it becomes especially important to choose foods that support your body's natural ability to recover. A diet filled with fresh fruits, colorful vegetables, lean proteins, and whole grains can give you all of the essential nutrients you need for your body to rebuild and function at its best. Eating nourishing foods helps regulate your blood sugar, reduce inflammation, and support your brain health—all of which are essential when you're continuously working through emotional and physical challenges.

It's also helpful to understand the connection between what you eat and how you feel afterward. Foods high in processed sugars, unhealthy fats, or caffeine can cause your blood sugar to rise quickly and then drop just as fast, causing you to feel crashed out. This is why that morning iced caramel latte and cheese danish from your local coffee shop isn't fueling you or keeping you energized. Sure, it's delicious in the moment, but give it an hour or two, and you'll be right back where you started—tired and grumpy. On the other hand, whole foods like leafy greens, berries, nuts, and seeds provide steady energy and help to keep your mind clear and calm. Eating balanced meals with protein, healthy fats, and fiber can stabilize your mood and improve focus throughout the day.

Planning out these meals doesn't have to be stressful, either. With AI, you can input a request to your phone or whatever program you use to give you not only a healthy meal plan but also all the recipes and a grocery list. In thirty seconds or less, you can have your entire week of meals planned out for you. There are no more excuses.

Just as mindful eating supports your recovery, staying hydrated plays a crucial role in how your body and mind function throughout the day. Water is essential for nearly every process in the body. It regulates temperature, aids digestion, delivers nutrients to cells, and cushions your joints. When you're hydrated, everything works more smoothly and with less friction. You might notice that you have more energy, better focus, and a more even mood. Even just mild dehydration can leave you feeling fatigued, with a headache and brain fog. There's no need to add extra weight to an already demanding healing process.

Reaching your hydration goal can be simple. Drinking water consistently throughout the day, rather than waiting until you're thirsty, is the most effective approach. Keeping a reusable water bottle nearby makes it easier to stay on track. You can increase hydration by eating water-rich foods like watermelon, oranges, strawberries, and cucumbers. Herbal teas or fruit-infused water with ingredients like lemon, mint, or berries can add flavor and make hydration more enjoyable. If you find drinking water difficult or unappealing, you can throw a pack of flavoring into your water to make it easier.

Shifting back to the mental health side of things, a digital detox offers a powerful opportunity to step away from screens and reconnect with what's in front of you. So much of our time is spent on social media, email, and constant scrolling, it is no surprise many people feel mentally drained and emotionally overwhelmed. Have you ever taken a moment to look at your screen time in the settings of your phone? It can be alarming to see a number over five, six, or even ten hours a day that you spend staring at your screen. The steady stream of notifications is feeding your anxiety, stress, and burnout.

The first step toward a meaningful digital detox is setting clear and realistic boundaries. Decide how long you want to take a break from your devices. This could be a few hours, an entire day, or a full weekend—just make sure it makes sense. If your screen time is currently twelve hours a day, you might not be successful if you reach for a forty-eight-hour detox immediately. In that case, start smaller, like with a six-hour detox. Pick a timeframe that feels manageable and supportive. If you rely on screens for work, try separating your work use from personal use. You can even set time limits for certain apps on your phone that you find yourself scrolling through or playing with too much. If you set your limit to one hour, don't be surprised if your apps lock at 10:00 a.m. when you've already spent your morning on your phone. It can be eye-opening.

Turn off unnecessary notifications, limit how often you check social media, and choose specific times to be offline. Something I did was take the time to color coordinate my apps, making them all dull and beige, and turning off all of those bright red notification bubbles that seemed to multiply endlessly on my home screen. This made looking at my phone much less stimulating, and I found it made me less anxiety-prone from seeing the bright colors and alerts. You can also create screen-free zones in your home, such as keeping phones out of the bedroom or off the dining table. These simple shifts can help you step away from constant digital interaction and reconnect with your surroundings.

As you move through your detox, pay close attention to how you feel both mentally and physically. The urge to check your phone might show up frequently at first. You've most likely developed the muscle memory of just pulling out your phone for no specific purpose, and choosing to stop yourself and put your phone back down will feel weird. The more frequently you do a digital detox, the faster that discomfort will subside.

This time away from screens can reveal how much influence technology has on your thoughts, energy, and daily choices. You'll find you most likely get out of bed much faster when there's nothing to scroll. You might become more productive at work or find you're taking more pleasure in the small moments with the people around you or even your pets. Use the experience to reflect on your current habits and consider what changes might support a more balanced and intentional life.

When your detox ends, return to digital life thoughtfully. Rather than falling back into old patterns, choose what habits are worth keeping. You might enjoy checking your phone less often, turning off certain notifications permanently, deleting particularly addictive apps, or just being more mindful about how and when you use your devices.

What you're really doing here isn't chasing perfection or trying to "fix" yourself. You're learning how to live in your body again, to listen when it speaks, to respond with care, and to build trust in your own rhythms. It's not always comfortable, but it's real. There's something powerful about choosing to show up for yourself, especially when you don't feel like it. These small, deliberate acts of self-care begin to stitch together a sense of stability, one that doesn't rely on having everything figured out.

As you start creating more structure in your life, it's less about discipline and more about returning to yourself, not the version of you shaped by pressure or survival but the version that feels calm, capable, and connected. You'll start to notice patterns, certain habits that leave you feeling more energized, and certain choices that lead to more ease. Use those moments as clues. They're pointing you toward the life that actually works for you.

There will still be days when things feel heavy, and that's okay. The goal isn't to eliminate hard days. It's to build a life where you know how to take care of yourself through them. When your routines are built on your own terms, when you're not chasing an image but instead honoring what your body and mind need, everything shifts. You stop striving for balance and start creating it, not because life suddenly gets easier but because you've given yourself the tools to meet it differently.

Chapter 6

Curating Motivation

Shaping Your Environment for Success

After trauma, motivation has a tendency to disappear in chunks. One day, you go from being someone who makes plans and follows through with everything on the calendar to someone who stares at a wall for hours or binge-watches a TV show from the moment you wake up to the moment you fall asleep. Despite what those around you (who are just trying their best to get you to do more) might say, it's not laziness or lack of ambition. Your brain and body just went through something massive, and they're trying to keep you alive—not productive. That's a hard thing to explain to people who haven't lived through what you have lived through. It's normal in this phase to start wondering *what the hell happened* to the version of you who used to care, used to try, and used to wake up with energy.

When you've been hurt and shaken to your core, especially if it's been over a longer period of time, your system gets wired to expect danger. So, instead of moving forward with focus or momentum, you freeze. You don't want to do anything. You hesitate. You wonder what the point is. Everything feels heavier than it should. The energy that used to go toward creating, planning, or dreaming now gets spent scanning for threats.

Imagine that you're having a quiet night at home, when suddenly you start to hear gunshots outside. What would you do? Maybe peek through your windows, turn your lights off, scan the yard and the streets, try and see what's going on. Then, you might lie in bed in this alert state, waiting to hear sirens or just waiting for more time to pass so that you feel like there isn't a threat anymore. That is the state of mind that you're in right now—no gunshots needed. You're on alert. Waiting for nothing. It's exhausting. Eventually, you stop trusting your ability to start things, let alone finish them, because you're too busy being frozen.

What often comes with this is a strange middle ground. Not a complete shutdown, but not real movement either. You might start to wake up a little, feeling flashes of clarity or energy, but they don't last too long. This is usually around the time that a lot of people really start to seek self-help, like picking up a book on trauma. You have enough energy to try mildly to recover.

It's an uncomfortable and weird in-between space where you want to care, you know you should care, and you want to do something productive to help, but every action feels like treading mud. You might get frustrated with yourself because *technically* nothing is wrong anymore. The crisis is over. The danger has passed. Yet you still can't make yourself move like you used to.

This is an emotionally gray zone of recovery. It's where survival mode is slowly starting to seep away but you haven't yet rebuilt the sense of safety that allows action to feel natural. You're caught between two identities: the version of you trying to protect themselves and survive and the version of you who knows you're going to be fine.

Another part of this phase that you might notice is the emotional flatness. You know what used to make you laugh, what used to excite you, what used to bring you comfort, but now it all feels the same. Flat. Even the things you *know* you love don't light you up anymore. It's confusing because on the surface, you look fine. You're getting through the day. You're functioning. But inside, everything feels dull and plain and muted. It's easier for your brain to keep things boring and predictable than to spark too much emotion. Energy means risk.

Soon, the guilt creeps in. You know that you're not functioning the way you used to, but you can't snap out of it. You know you should be doing more, but you don't have the bandwidth. That's where the spiral begins. One layer of internal pressure turns into a stack that keeps building until everything feels impossible. The longer you stay there, the easier it becomes to believe that maybe this is just how life is now, and the person that you used to be isn't coming back. This is the new you.

This is all normal and a part of the process. That older version of you is still there, just waiting in the shadows (peeking through the curtains, if you will) waiting for that danger level to drop, even when the danger is long gone. They're waiting to feel safe enough to show up again. Now, you're in a place where you can begin creating the conditions for yourself that allow you to return. It's time to get out of bed and stop staring at the ceiling. We're looking for that spark again.

When you've lived in this state of survival for so long, it takes time for your body to believe that safety is real again. You can tell yourself a thousand times that you are fine, but your nervous system will still flinch with uncertainty. Your body has memorized what it feels like to be in danger. The tight chest, the shallow breath, the racing thoughts, and now it's trying to unlearn that pattern.

Healing means retraining that internal system, little by little, to stop bracing for an imaginary impact. Your body has to experience calm and peace repeatedly before it trusts on its own again. This is why creating an environment that feels so grounded and predictable is particularly powerful.

Safety starts with familiarity. Drinking your coffee from the same mug every morning. Making your bed. Playing the same show every night when you cook dinner. These are patterns that seem insignificant, but they are gestures that make your body and mind feel comfortable and naturally at ease. Like you are in control again.

We know healing from trauma requires emotional work (obviously), but it also requires a supportive environment, one that will nurture your daily motivation and encourage progress. You might think motivation is a fast burst of inspiration, which is definitely true in some cases, but it can also come from shaping your surroundings in a way that naturally propels you forward. When your environment is aligned with your goals, it becomes much easier to stay on track and build momentum over time.

It's pretty common sense that you're going to feel more upbeat and motivated when you're in an environment that allows you to relax and enjoy things, as opposed to a high-emotion, unorganized, and stressful environment. Being in a happy space allows your mind to rest and explore things. It's the same reason people go on vacation, to escape whatever reality and stressors they have at home.

The first step you can take to curate your environment and surroundings is to look at the things you consume. Not physically, but mentally. I'm talking about your digital world. Completing the digital detox was the first step, but it's important to also curate your digital environment to be supportive when you aren't detoxing.

The content you consume daily on your phone, computer, or TV is probably affecting you much more than you think. The human mind is not made to process the world's tragedies at 8:00 a.m. while you're having breakfast. Following the news so closely, scrolling on apps that might not have the best regulations (allowing really anything to pop up), along with constantly comparing yourself to people online, shapes your thoughts, moods, and energy much more than you realize. You should never start your day or spend your afternoon looking at social media feeds that are filled with negativity, unrealistic expectations, politics, or posts that leave you feeling moody or drained. Just like decluttering a physical environment can bring you relief and clarity, filtering what you see online can create a healthier, more positive, and motivating atmosphere.

When was the last time you actually clicked on your *follow* list and looked at who you were following on social media? Has it been months or even years? Have you ever even actually done that? It's so easy to accumulate connections, old classmates, distant relatives, influencers, even people you don't know or remember why you were following. When you have the time, truly go through that list. Ask yourself: Does their content still serve you? Are you still enjoying their posts, or has what started as "keeping up with and staying in touch" turned into a daily spiral of complaints, rage, bragging, or unrealistic expectations?

Set some boundaries here. You don't have to unfollow everyone (especially if they might be the type of person to take it personally), but most platforms have a "mute" button for a reason. It lets you completely remove certain energies from your feed without cutting ties completely. You can still greet those people warmly if you run into them in public, but you don't have to hear about their political views or champagne problems every day. You don't have to sift through someone's passive-aggressive posts or constant brags and complaints just because you knew them in high school or share DNA. Keeping them on your feed out of guilt or obligation doesn't make you loyal; it just makes your online space more emotionally chaotic.

Ask yourself honestly, do you even want to become the kind of person who spends their time broadcasting negativity or bragging about things that don't align with your true values? Probably not. So, why give that energy front-row access to your day? Constantly seeing people behave in ways that you disagree with, especially when it stirs judgment, annoyance, or insecurity, doesn't challenge your perspective in a productive way. It just wears you down. You are allowed total control to curate that part of your world. You are allowed to protect your peace. You don't need to stay emotionally entangled with every thought, opinion, or update that crosses your screen. Let yourself detach. Not everything needs your reaction, and not everyone needs your attention. What *does* need your attention right now is the journey of growth and healing that you are on.

Make your social media a place that uplifts, encourages, and motivates you. Follow accounts that make you feel good. Follow people with bodies that look like yours. Brands you love. People who have the same goals as you. Friends and family who actually brighten your day. Influencers who take your mind off stress, not add to it. Instead of you mindlessly scrolling and feeling worse, your feed can be curated to give you constant encouragement, ideas, and subtle reminders of who you want to become.

I know firsthand how important this is. When I was deep in my own healing journey, trying to process and recover from sexual assault, I hated my body. I didn't want to look at it. It was painful, and I felt ugly all the time. One of the strongest and most important shifts I made was unfollowing influencers whose bodies didn't look like mine. Constant comparison was tearing me down every day, and I wanted a strong enough mindset to be able to look at those people and just enjoy their content without strictly wishing my body looked like theirs. When I started following women with bodies like mine, women who were confident and stylish and unbothered, it made a huge change for me. I didn't feel so out of place anymore. I started seeing beauty where I hadn't before. I saw that people who looked like me were able to feel confident and wear the pretty clothing and be social without fear. That change in my digital world gave me permission to start seeing myself through a softer, more accepting lens. That's how powerful your environment can be, even when it's just the one on your screen.

Curating motivation in your digital world is just the beginning. While it's a powerful step toward building a better mindset, major changes need to happen in your physical world, too. Your environment plays a huge role in your emotions, stability, and behavior. When your space is noisy, cluttered, or chaotic, it creates this undercurrent of stress that makes everything from small tasks to big goals feel harder than they need to. It drains your energy before you even begin, making it easy to feel overwhelmed or unmotivated without fully understanding why. Your external world is often a direct reflection of your internal world, and vice versa.

That said, there will always be parts of your environment that are completely out of your control. Maybe you have a neighbor who slams doors at odd hours, a baby who needs you constantly, or roommates who are always leaving messes behind. Those things are real, and they can be frustrating, but staying angry at them won't move you forward. Resentment toward your environment will only keep you feeling exhausted and unwilling to move forward. It's easy to use those factors as an excuse for why you can't be happy, but it's toxic to do so.

Your power lies in focusing on what is directly within your reach. Maybe that means creating a small corner where you work, using noise-canceling earbuds, adjusting the layout of a shared room, or setting small rituals that give you peace, even when the rest of the space feels completely out of sync. These changes signal to your brain that you're choosing peace wherever you can.

On the other hand, a clean and peaceful space gives you clarity and control, which helps you stay focused. Look around at the spaces where you spend the most time. Where you wake up, where you work, and where you relax. Do these areas feel functional and calm, or do they leave you tense and scattered? Do you know where everything is, or do you tend to spend time searching and cleaning before you can even start your day?

Simplifying your space can shift your mindset immediately. Think about that moment after a full afternoon of cleaning, when a candle is lit, the wine is poured, and you finally sink into the couch. That's the feeling we're chasing here. You shouldn't be holding on to things that are just taking up space and collecting dust. Keep what's necessary, meaningful, or brings you happiness. A thoughtfully arranged space helps you breathe easier and feel more in control. It clears the mental clutter alongside the physical, giving you more energy to focus on what really matters.

I'm not telling you that you have to be an all-out minimalist, although I definitely consider myself one. I understand that the idea can feel overwhelming or impractical for most people. Still, there are simple parts of that mindset that anyone can benefit from.

Minimalism, at its core, means being more intentional with the things that you allow in your space. It's asking questions like, "Do I even like this?" or, "Why am I even holding on to this?" You don't need to toss everything or live out of a suitcase to create calm in your home. Just a small decision, like clearing off a surface or letting go of a pile of clothes you haven't worn in years, can create more space both physically and mentally. The goal is to make room for the version of you that you're becoming, rather than staying buried in the leftovers of who you used to be.

Your workspace especially matters. Whether it's a desk at home or the office, clutter pulls your attention to every detail. Piles of paper, scattered supplies and unread emails . . . all of it adds noise. Digital clutter is just as exhausting. Your phone, for example, might look harmless on the surface, but when it's overloaded with dozens of apps in a thousand different colors, it becomes a constant source of low-level chaos. If every time you unlock your phone you're hit with a carnival of bright, mismatched icons and red notification dots, you're triggering your brain to scan, decide, and react, even when you're not consciously aware of it. The overstimulation adds up fast.

Start by reorganizing your phone the same way you would a junk drawer. You don't have to delete everything. Most phones allow you to simply "remove from home screen" so that the app is still there but no longer in your face. Out of sight, out of mind. You can search for it if you really need it. If you're feeling extra motivated, you can take it a step further and color-code your home screen or even tone it all down to neutrals or a single, calming color palette. You don't need your phone to feel like a neon circus every time you pick it up. Treat your phone like an extension of your space, not just something that is constantly pulling your attention away from everything else.

Just as a cluttered room can leave you feeling chaotic, a crowded closet can do the same. An overflowing wardrobe filled with clothes you don't wear turns getting dressed into a stressor. Let go of what no longer fits, doesn't suit you, or makes you feel *blah*. One of the biggest mental weights hiding in your closet is the pile of "someday" clothes. I'm talking about the jeans you haven't worn in five years or the dress you've been saving for when your body magically turns back into what it was at eighteen. Holding on to those pieces might seem harmless, but they're sending you a silent message every day that who you are right now isn't good enough and that you're waiting for a version of yourself that might not even feel good when you get there.

You deserve a wardrobe that fits the life and body you have today, clothes that celebrate where you are, not guilt for where you aren't.

When you open your closet and see only things that fit, flatter, and reflect your current style, you're able to start your day feeling seen and supported, not delayed and defeated. Those "one day" pieces aren't motivating. They're mothballing away while you're self-worth quietly erodes under their weight. You don't need to shrink back into who you were. You need to make room for who you are becoming.

Sensory cues like sound, scent, texture and light all play roles in how your brain processes comfort, focus, and stress. When you intentionally design your space with these in mind, you create an atmosphere that supports your energy.

Start with sound. Some people need silence to think clearly, while others work best with music, a fan, or ambient background noise. It's a detail that is personal and is often overlooked. If you live in a noisy household or apartment, even a small adjustment like noise-canceling earbuds or a white noise machine can create a shift in your focus. If total silence feels unsettling, try low-volume instrumental music or something steady and neutral like a cafe playlist, fireplace crackle, or rainfall. Over time, that sound becomes a signal to your brain that it is time to settle in. It sets the tone for your mindset. When the noise around you settles, your mind has more space to engage, create, and follow through.

Smell is another simple but powerful tool that often goes unnoticed and unused. Scents have a direct link to the part of the brain that controls emotion and memory. It's why sometimes you smell something and you're suddenly taken back to a specific place or environment or even moment where you knew that smell. A citrus candle can lift you up, giving you a fresh mental start in the morning. Earthy or floral oils can help you wind down after a stressful day. You don't need some perfect and overwhelming fragrance, just a subtle scent that makes you feel a little calmer, clearer, and more focused. Having a candle or an essential oil diffuser might not scream motivation, but it supports you more than you know in setting the right mood.

Something you might not have considered is texture. Texture plays a bigger role in motivation than people give it credit for. You might not think much about a throw blanket or a soft rug, but your body notices. Your nervous system responds to comfort, and that response shapes how much energy you have for other tasks. A stiff chair or a cluttered surface might not seem like a big deal, but when you're already tired, burnt out, or just feeling off, discomfort becomes one more reason to avoid starting. Add softness wherever you can. A cozy chair, a comfortable pair of slippers, or a thick blanket might seem like small comforts, but they help create an environment that is easy to settle into. When your body feels at ease in your space, it is simpler to stay present and focused and to get things done.

Lighting also affects your energy and pace. Natural light is one of the most reliable sources of focus and energy, but it's not always available. Bright, cool-toned lights can wake you up and help with productivity during the day. Warmer, dimmer lights slow you down and help you relax when it's time to rest. Even if your space is limited, a simple lamp or color-adjustable bulb can help create the right mood for the moment. When your surroundings support your internal rhythm, staying motivated becomes less about forcing effort and more about working with what already feels right.

Start with the small details. A framed photo, a few plants, a favorite print, or even a stack of books can make your space feel more personal and grounded. A handwritten quote near your desk or a family photo in view can quietly pull you back to your purpose. These subtle cues are there to gently remind you of who you are and what matters most. Sometimes, that quiet reinforcement is all it takes to bring your focus back.

This is where micro-moments can make a difference. Motivation can easily stem from a small choice. Something minimal enough to overlook but meaningful enough to shift your direction. Do things like stretching for one minute instead of picking up your phone when you need a moment away from what you're doing. Change out of your pajamas. Light a candle before you start. Open the blinds when you don't feel like it. These tiny actions are declarations that today matters, and you are going to show up for it.

What most people fail to realize is that tiny actions are how you rebuild trust with yourself. Every time you follow through with something, no matter how small, you're proving you can rely on your own effort. You build faith in your own consistency.

Think about the feeling that comes after you finally finish one small thing you've been avoiding—washing dishes, taking out the trash, or sending an email. It's not the size of the task that matters; it's the signal it sends. You showed up. You did something. That flicker of accomplishment plants a seed of momentum. Motivation can really grow in those small and ordinary victories. Over time, those micro-moments start to reshape your identity back to where you want it to be. You begin to trust that you are someone who can follow through again. This shift is huge. It changes the tone of your self-talk, the way you approach each day, even the energy you bring into your space. Progress stops being something you have to chase and starts being something you create on your own through small, steady choices.

When you're healing, micro-moments like these matter more than ever, they're the building blocks of your new routine, your new self, your new normal. Even if you're not ready to do the big thing—go for a run, clean the whole house, clean out the garage—you can still do something small. One small intentional choice leads to another.

A reliable way to make a new habit stick is by connecting it to something you already do regularly. This approach, called habit stacking, uses your current routine as a foundation. Instead of trying to create time or space out of nowhere, the idea is to tuck in a new habit into a spot that already exists. You're working with the natural rhythm of your day. These connections and habits are like little cues that help guide your next move without needing a ton of energy or thought.

One thing that has worked really well for me is my nighttime routine. I always keep my current book and my journal on my nightstand. Since they're already sitting there, I don't have to go looking for them or remind myself to use them or talk myself into anything. Once I get into bed, I just reach for them. I write a few things in my journal, then read until I start to feel sleepy. It's not a big chore to set that up for myself, and because it is so easy and consistent, it happens without me having to think about it. That simple setup made the habit stick.

If you make coffee every morning, leave your journal or your vitamins next to the machine and journal while your coffee brews. If you always shower after your evening walk, set out your skincare or pajamas before you leave. Little setups like this cut down the gap between what you want to do and actually doing it. The next step is already waiting for you, so instead of forcing yourself into action, you're just following a path that you've already laid out.

Each time you follow through, it takes a little less effort. The habit starts to feel more natural, like something you just do. Over time, these pairings create structure. Not a rigid routine, but a steady path that fits into your life. It becomes easier to be consistent because you're not working against yourself every step of the way.

Start small, especially when you're trying to create new rhythms after a difficult season in your life. You don't need a 10-step morning routine or a full reset to make progress. You just need one small habit that connects to something you already do. These little pairings are simple enough to repeat and light enough to not feel like a chore. That's the whole point. You get the idea. You're not trying to overhaul your life all at one, you're creating small links that are easy to maintain, even when your energy is low. With repetition, they stop feeling like something you have to do and start becoming a part of what you're already doing. That's how momentum builds effortlessly.

Perfectionism is going to try and get in the way. When you're healing or worn down, tiny setbacks feel huge. That voice that says "I'll just start over next week" might sound logical, but most of the time it's just a way to avoid discomfort. Making a mistake doesn't mean you've failed and that you need to start over again. It just means that your brain is still fighting you and trying to protect you from something that feels hard. Missing a day doesn't cancel out your progress, but choosing to start all over again sure does. It's what you do *after* you made a mistake that really matters.

Some days, even the smallest task is going to feel like a lot. That's okay. It doesn't mean you're back at square one, it just means you need a little more flexibility and care that day. When an error happens, bring your focus in close. Do things that help you feel grounded. Make your bed slowly. Fold some clothes. Wipe of your counter. Water your plants. Do things that aren't necessarily glamorous but make you feel like you are still tending to your environment and being steady.

A lot of the time, your motivation will be something you build by repeating little choices that seem unimportant in the moment but shape how you move through the day. When your space feels calm, your systems actually work for your life, and your routines don't exhaust you, everything gets a little easier. You don't have to constantly push yourself forward because you've created something that can carry you, even on the harder days. That's where real change lives, in the foundation you build and the consistency you keep showing up for.

Once motivation starts to return, the goal will shift from finding it to keeping it steady. It's easy to forget that motivation is alive. It changes with your seasons, your stress levels, and your needs. You'll have weeks where it feels like pulling teeth, and weeks where it will feel natural. The key is to learn to notice when the spark is fading and being able to do some adjusting before it burns out.

Pay attention to early warning signs that you might be backtracking. When everything starts to feel heavy again, when clutter is building up again, when you stop preparing for your routines and doing things that you know make you feel good. Those are your cues to recalibrate. Go back to the basics—clean a surface, reset a routine, take a walk, light a candle, or even walk around your house with a trash bag and make yourself fill it up. Your motivation is still there; it's just hiding under all the noise.

You'll never completely master motivation; you'll just figure it out more and get better at maintaining it. The more you check in with yourself and your environment, the easier it becomes to keep that foundation solid. Motivation is something you must tend to, like a garden. Some days it will thrive without much effort; other days you'll need to pull weeds, spray with pesticide, re-mulch, and water it. The more you nurture it through care, awareness, and small daily choices, the stronger it grows, weathers the seasons, and remains.

Chapter 7

Transforming Your Career
Finding Purpose and Fulfillment

As you start to rebuild your motivation, you'll notice a difference in the way you perceive your daily life. You'll notice the energy drains and the habits or routines that no longer work in your favor. You'll be able to break down the pieces of your day that now somehow feel out of sync with the future you're building. When you consider that you spend more than one-third of your life in the workplace, it's no surprise that one of the biggest areas where misalignment will show up for you is your career.

Some days at work feel heavier than others. You wake up, you get out of bed, you get dressed, you eat breakfast, and you clock in at your normal time—but it doesn't feel like you're actually there. You're simply going through the motions. What was once effortless for you now feels incredibly draining. It takes even more energy just to speak. Recalling small things or answering questions about procedures you once knew so well and had memorized now takes a little more gas in the tank to figure out. At this point, you're wading through the mud of recovery, and existing in this manner each day requires a lot more energy than the people around you will understand.

There is a big difference between functioning and coping. You can still be getting all your tasks done, managing emails, and completing reports, but beneath the surface, you are struggling to remain above water. Most of your coworkers won't ever figure this out, especially if you're adept at concealing any stress or emotions. Your boss will still ask you to do more work. You're still going to receive compliments or praise for performing well—and the only person who might really know how close you are to toppling is you. You quit trying to survive, and you simply try to stay upright. When you're in this state, even tiny gestures of kindness can feel like lifelines.

Certain coworkers will enter your work life and be the only reason you can breathe during a grueling workweek. These are not going to be the friends you have in-depth conversations with or drink martinis on a Friday night with, but they will be there for you simply because you spend forty hours a week together. Their support might show up in a silly text during the day that makes you laugh or even by saving a seat for you at a meeting because they know you're running on empty.

These are the coworkers who simplify your day and make it more palatable. These work relationships are the best kind. They're usually built on a foundation of shared frustrations or angst, or possibly even because you were griping about the same person in the break room. It might not be the strongest foundation, but having them around keeps your feet on the ground.

They listen when something feels off about you. They check on you when you've gone quiet. You don't feel you owe them your whole story to receive companionship or support. That steady, low-profile support is what everyone needs at work. Some of these relationships fade after you leave a job. Others continue in group chats, spur-of-the-moments catch-ups, or even lengthy voice messages. Temporary or not, those connections are important. During tough times and loneliness, small gestures count. Try to pinpoint these people in your work environment, and pull them close—lean on them when you need to be rebalanced.

Meanwhile, all the extra labor you put in to just seem normal will go unnoticed. From the outside, staying steady, pushing through, and holding it together just seems like a normal day-to-day routine. Remember that your persistence in continuing to show up and do the job is meaningful, even when it goes without praise. On the worst days, just being present is proof of your strength and resilience. This, however, can be a double-edged sword. The resilience you've gotten so good at proving can quickly be mistaken for ease by the people around you.

When people get used to seeing you powering through, check-ins vanish. Expectations rise. You go from being the person who was consistent and reliable to being the person people depend on. Adjectives like *reliable* and *quick-witted* begin to show up when describing your character, dressed as praise but in reality being load-bearing. Overload is overlooked because it's assumed that you have everything under control. Because of this, you force yourself to continue—not out of confidence but out of fear of what might happen if your reliability rhythm breaks.

There's a high cost to the composure you're constantly keeping. You're training your mind to default to emotional restraint. Tears are held back during meetings or calls, and breakdowns are saved for private moments. You convince yourself that you are not allowed to show any form of vulnerability because showing emotions at work can alter the perception of your competence. In most work environments, when you're openly emotional, you're going to be seen as someone unable to carry their position. Nobody wishes to give an employee a raise or promotion when they go out of their way to make it clear that they are not emotionally composed. This way of thinking gives you additional reason to keep everything under wraps. There is too high of a risk for miscommunication, so it seems wiser to just maintain your guard.

For most people (especially those going through the healing process), the job you do when you begin to cater to your own needs is not the job you're meant to stay with. Your job might have been something you chose for survival, or maybe you defaulted into it because you knew you could land the position and needed the money.

As you start to feel stronger and more steady, you'll naturally want more out of your life. More peace. More meaning. More fulfillment. Better relationships. Healthier, more enjoyable circumstances. That's a good sign. It means you're moving forward.

Your job is part of your healing whether you like it or not. It isn't something you can box off while you focus on everything else. Work affects your stress, your stability, and your sense of progress. At the same time, your rent, mortgage, and bills won't pause because you're working through trauma. They still have to be paid. That reality doesn't make you weak. It just means healing has to happen alongside real life, not outside of it.

Certain work cultures can activate parts of you that you might not feel you can manage yet. You might find yourself reacting to things at work more intensely than they warrant, or you might check out mentally when doing something that requires dedicated attention. Your nervous system can't always differentiate the real threat from past associations, so a yelling boss, being shut down in the middle of a conversation, or receiving some unexpected or negative feedback on your work can all be triggers for large reactions from you.

Over-functioning can look like commitment. Freezing can look like indecision. Fawning can look like being easygoing and agreeable. On the outside, some of these traits even get praised. The problem is that they're exhausting to keep up. If you've spent years learning how to avoid conflict or stay small to feel safe, that pattern doesn't just disappear. You carry it with you into every new workplace, even when the original threat is no longer there.

The first step to transforming and correcting is to observe. If your stomach sinks when you enter a meeting or you find yourself getting teary after an email, that's your warning sign.

You don't need to cope with or correct these things in the moment, just note them for yourself. You aren't expected to be an emotionless robot at work (at least I hope you aren't). The goal is to become conscious of what is going on inside so you can act from choice rather than emotion. In time, your ability to remain calm when faced with stress will become easier.

At the same time, your work should never get in the way of your healing. When emotional pain is more than you can handle, it can be tempting to take refuge in your work. You can fill every spare moment with overtime, new tasks, or an endless list of things to do so you don't have time to think, but that's not the best route to take.

It might feel like you're making progress, but fleeing from your thoughts with work is different from making progress. When you work overtime instead of making time for healing, you are hiding behind overachieving. It's the perfect way to feel good about yourself and the money you're making and keep yourself from quiet moments when it's just you and your thoughts. Don't be fooled. If your job consumes so much time that you never sit with your feelings, then it's a barrier and not a solution.

Healing requires space. It requires quiet. No amount of productivity or achievement can replace the inner calm your body actually needs.

Most people don't realize how much their work environment affects their nervous system. Trauma gets stored in the body, and even long after the original event, your system can stay on high alert. Then you add forty or more hours a week in a place that still triggers you, and your body never truly gets a break.

Maybe it's the unpredictability of your boss's mood. Maybe it's the requirement to respond instantly to every email you receive. Maybe it's because your needs are always disrespected and ignored, even when you give your all. Not only does this give you stress, but it also tells your body you have not yet found safety, as evidenced by your exhaustion, tension, irritability, or emotional shutdown. It's easy to normalize that atmosphere. Maybe you tell yourself all jobs are stressful, or someone told you this is "just how work is"—but if your body is telling you it doesn't feel safe, you need to listen. Whether you stay in your current position or not, you owe it to yourself to be honest. Is your work healing you or hurting you?

It's frustrating and frightening to know your role no longer fits, especially when you feel like you have to stay. It's foreign territory for many. Maybe the perks are tremendous, or you feel you've built the place from the ground up. Maybe you know so many people are proud of you for having the job that you have. Maybe the thought of starting over elsewhere is overwhelming. You know deep down that you've outgrown the work, but walking away would mean giving up more than just a paycheck—it would mean stepping into the unknown without a guarantee that something better is waiting.

That in-between period is suffocating. You're grateful to be working, but you're also bitter about all it's taking away. You fantasize about quitting, then feel guilty because there are people worse off than you. You write resignation letters in your head but keep logging in every morning. Holding two things at the same time: appreciation and discontent. How confusing is that? Here's the thing—work is where you earn money, but it's also a component of who you are, what your daily life looks like, and your emotional well-being. If you value healing, your career needs to be considered.

If someone told you that they could tell how much you love yourself by the job you have, would it feel like an insult, or a compliment? Here's your sign.

You can't keep giving the largest parts of your week to a place that is counteracting the healing and growth you're doing when not at work. How do you feel after your workday? Proud of yourself? At ease when you're there? Are your boundaries honored? Does your work match your values, or does it drag you into patterns that feel comfortable and stagnant? Even worse, are you so thrilled to be done with the workday that you get into your car, let out a long sigh, and have to mentally reset for your evening? That uneasiness is data. It's pointing you toward clarity. It's a big red flashing sign that says, *Stop doing this.* You need honesty and realignment in order to grow. It's time to be honest with yourself about what you might have outgrown.

Not every job is tearing you down, but a lot of them are misaligned—and that misalignment looks like burnout, anxiety, and disengagement. We stay in those jobs because it's easy and they're comfortable. Because they suit the version of us we've always been. Because they protect us from the danger of change. Unfortunately, though, the path of growth you're on might require you to leave behind a position that made sense before.

Your career doesn't have to be your one big great passion. You don't have to be obsessed with all assignments or uncover some of your soul in all the emails you send. What is important is that your work allows you to feel well and does not cost you more than it benefits you, that it lets you live with dignity, room, and solidity. Not all professions are meaningful. Sometimes you just need something humane that allows you to grow.

I'm not suggesting you don't pursue your dreams or a job that is your passion. If that's what calls to you, you should go for it. You spend at least a third of your life at work, so if you need to have the job you've always wanted to feel significant and valuable, then you should. Just make sure you're not doing the opposite—staying in an environment that's toxic and unhealthy because you have told yourself it is your passion.

For example, if it's always been your dream to be a screenwriter but you find yourself working eighty hours a week and exhausted and miserable, yet you're doing it because film has always been your passion and now you have the opportunity, you probably need to reconsider. You need to find the middle ground: doing something you enjoy in a healthy environment.

When you find yourself needing to quit a job, even when it's unsuitable and you know it's not the one for you, it can cause a wide range of emotions. It's easy to expect the relief of knowing that you won't have to deal with the people or the workload anymore. What you might also feel, however, is a strange sense of loss, almost like you've lost a part of yourself. We spend so long at work, after all, that it really does become part of us and our identity.

Whether the environment was good or bad, that job shaped your everyday life. Leaving can feel like breaking a promise you once made to yourself, especially to an earlier version of you who wanted that role so badly or felt proud to land it.

Change often comes with grief, especially when your identity is shifting. You can feel thankful for what a job gave you and still admit that it limited your growth. Both can be true at the same time.

It's normal to question your instincts, even when you sense they're right. You'll second-guess decisions. You'll hold back ideas. What looks like hesitation is often your nervous system learning that it's finally safe to speak up.

One of the best ways to rebuild trust in yourself is to notice where you're already getting it right. Maybe you send the email without rereading it five times. Maybe you share your opinion in a meeting. Maybe you set a boundary with someone who usually pushes back. Those small moments matter. They're proof that your instincts still work. They've just been buried under self-doubt for a while.

In a lot of workplaces, setting boundaries can feel a lot harder than it should. Letting people know when you're at your limit can bring up a lot of worries about being labeled difficult or uncooperative. In environments that praise nonstop productivity and look down on being thorough or taking a break, setting a boundary can feel like you're doing something rebellious. Saying no to extra tasks or standing your ground often comes with guilt or anxiety, even when it's the most sensible thing to do.

Boundaries at work can be as basic as not responding to messages outside of work hours, remaining emotionally separate from a constant complainer, or fighting the temptation to volunteer when your work-week has been full. Making these decisions might feel uncomfortable initially, but that doesn't mean they're not the right choices. You still have to protect your own peace. Assertiveness in the workplace is awkward because it challenges your need to feel worthy. You have to start to retrain your mind to not feel wrong for expressing yourself clearly. Being direct does not mean you are rude or heartless, and being able to say no is not an indication that you lack a work ethic.

Boundaries are how you stay faithful to what you can do and what you can't do. Without them, burnout is pretty much inevitable. In that way, your work can be a tool for identity repair. Most people after trauma feel like they've lost themselves. They've lost their voice, their confidence, or even their sense of direction. The right work environment can help you put those pieces back together. Every time you get a task done, help a colleague, try something new, or fix a problem, you're showing yourself that you're capable, valuable, and independent. Those small victories, even when they feel mundane, are actually scaffolding for your new self.

One area in which healing shows up at work is in how you manage emotional boundaries. When you're still untangling trauma, emotions can overspill easily. You might cry at your workstation, snap at a coworker, or say more than you meant to. It's normal to want connection in tough times. It's normal to want care, but not all environments are prepared to support your vulnerable moments.

This is where the concept of trauma dumping is important to understand. The term *trauma dumping* means unprocessed pain suddenly, or in abundance, dumping into spaces that aren't prepared to take it. It happens when we have nowhere else to place our anger or sadness, so we lay it on the nearest people available, which could be a colleague, a boss, or a team. You're spending at least forty hours a week with these people, so it seems obvious that they're going to learn a lot about your personal life in the process. While it might feel relieving in the moment, discussing trauma at work rarely leads to real support. Instead, it can create discomfort, distance, or confusion. Your coworkers might care about you, but they're not your therapist.

Your workplace, no matter how friendly the culture is or how welcoming the people are, is not a replacement for emotional processing. Your coworkers might tell you they feel sorry for you or they might sympathize with you for a while, but this is just so they can continue on with their workday before heading home and complaining to their spouse about you letting your emotions dictate the workday. People have boundaries, and a lot of people are not trying to make friends at work. They just want to be your coworker. Your emotions do not need to be suppressed, but they do need the right container. They need to be released in purposeful spaces like therapy, friendship, or a caring community where feelings can come to rest and be received with compassion by people who are expecting it.

When you safeguard the workplace from the responsibility of having to handle people with unprocessed pain, a more respectful and fair space is preserved. This allows professionalism and peace to coexist. Support in the workplace doesn't always appear as sharing on a personal level. It's found at times in visibility.

When emotional safety is respected in a workplace, people are less likely to seek relief through trauma dumping because the environment itself models healthy containment. This often starts at the top. Leaders who have done their own healing work and know how to hold boundaries with empathy set the tone for everyone else. They understand that care doesn't always mean oversharing, and support doesn't require personal disclosure to be genuine. When leadership demonstrates emotional maturity, it creates a culture where people can express humanity without spilling over, where compassion and composure can coexist. In those spaces, others feel seen without having to expose their pain to be understood.

It's easier to believe in yourself when you can see someone else already standing where you're trying to go. That might be a woman in leadership, a leader with a story that sounds like yours, or a colleague who speaks honestly and plainly. Those kinds of people don't just inspire you. They create a sense of safety.

Belonging starts to feel possible instead of uncertain. When those examples are missing, the path can feel lonelier and much harder to climb.

You might find yourself questioning things and wondering if you need to become someone different to be that strong person in leadership. Maybe you feel like you need to tone yourself down, adjust your personality, or even talk less because the place you're in does not reflect anything you know. That sort of disconnection can whittle your confidence.

If you have not met someone like yourself in the career you desire, that doesn't mean you're reaching for too much. It just means you need to pave the way. You don't need to earn your way into acceptance. You can do things differently without it making you less qualified or less needed. When someone stands in front of the room and makes space for others to see themselves in that position, it really matters.

For some, healing also leads to a deeper question: what if you're not meant to work for someone else at all? Entrepreneurship is not just a business decision. To many people, especially those emerging from careers where they were controlled, silenced, or diminished, it's a risky and liberating choice. Having the ability to create your own work, your own tempo, and your own purpose offers more than financial freedom. It offers the opportunity to create a space that represents your values, your spirit, and your needs. Entrepreneurship is not easy. It's isolating, uncertain, and filled with stress of its own. But it's also filled with a lot of potential.

When you pursue entrepreneurship, you get to decide what your work will be like. You get to create systems that benefit your well-being. You get to build your identity based not on compliance but on creativity and agency. You get to set your own rules and values in your own company, and you get to make sure everything aligns. You get to create an environment for other people to work in—the one you have always been looking for.

If your healing journey has brought you to the idea of working for yourself, you don't necessarily have to know everything right away. You just have to listen to that and begin exploring it. There is a component here that's important to note, and it's called ambition.

A lot of people healing from trauma have an issue with wanting more. It can feel unfamiliar, even dangerous, to crave expansion after years spent surviving. You might assume that having a lot of ambition is greedy, unsafe, unstable, unrealistic, or even selfish. You might have been taught that security is found in modesty or that wanting more than what you have means you're ungrateful.

Maybe people around you roll their eyes at your ideas or treat your dreams like something fragile and far-fetched. They might think your goals are a little bit silly, that you shouldn't be dreaming that big, that success like this belongs to someone else. When you've been conditioned to play small, desire itself starts to feel like rebellion. The safer choice seems to be staying quiet, staying comfortable, staying predictable. The solution to that line of thinking is to just quit, conform, and stay safe right where you are—though deep down, you know that kind of safety comes at the cost of your growth.

This kind of thinking is what keeps people stuck in places they've already outgrown. It convinces you that comfort and peace are the same thing. It's the hesitation that says it's better not to try than to risk failing, even when part of you wants more. Staying small can feel safe at first. Over time, though, that kind of safety stops protecting you and starts confining you.

Wanting a promotion, a new job title, more pay, or even a whole new path—like pursuing entrepreneurship or a personal passion—isn't arrogance. It's the soul's way of reminding you that you're still alive, still capable of more than just surviving. Those desires are flickers of light in the night, calling you toward the next version of yourself, even when you can't yet see what it looks like.

When you start believing in your abilities again, when that small thought shows up that says maybe I can do this, you're not being unrealistic. You're stepping into who you're becoming. Success can feel unfamiliar after a hard season. Even when things start going well, there can be a strange tension underneath it. You might brace for it to fall apart. You might wonder if you really deserve it. You might even worry that it could disappear or that someone else will resent you for having it. Those feelings can sit in the background without running your life. Let them be there without handing them control. Never allow someone else's resentment to decide how much space you take up or how much credit you give yourself.

The truth is, your growth doesn't take anything away from anyone else. Your stability, your progress, your success do not need to be explained or justified to the people around you.

You can feel grateful and still admit that it feels a little unfamiliar. You're allowed to appreciate the life you're building, even if it looks nothing like the one you came from. You don't owe anyone an apology for changing your circumstances. What you've worked for isn't luck, and you don't have to shrink it just because someone else feels uncomfortable.

What you don't change, you choose.

As you consider what you're going to do next, think about what type of work would feed you rather than just exhaust you. Picture what it would feel like to end your day with a sense of pride instead of depletion—to feel stimulated, challenged, and fulfilled instead of drained. Think about whether the job you're in truly reflects the version of you that you're becoming or if it represents an older version of you that you've already outgrown.

Ask yourself what quiet beliefs you're carrying about what's possible and where those beliefs came from. Are they yours, or did someone hand them to you years ago? Consider what identity you're reinforcing by remaining in your current situation—what story you're telling yourself each day by staying there. Then ask what would shift if you gave yourself full permission to want something different. Sometimes, that single act of permission is what begins to rebuild your faith in what's still possible for you.

Let your work resemble your growth. Let it leave space for your values, your strength, and your vision. Whether you are early or advanced in your career, you are allowed to make different choices. It is never too late to get up and walk away from something that has been slowly killing you. It's one of the most exciting things about life—that you get to design a future that feels good to live in, not just good to look at.

Chapter 8

Finding Independence

Managing the Balance of Alone and Together

When you throw yourself fully into your work, it can feel like the most empowering thing in the world. There's deep satisfaction in knowing you can take care of yourself, pay your own bills, and build a life you want without relying on anybody else. Yet underneath that freedom, there's often something more complicated happening in the back of your mind, especially for people carrying old wounds.

Many of us learned early that the only person we could truly rely on was ourselves. Maybe it came from a betrayal that taught you to keep your guard up. Maybe it came from a childhood where asking for help meant you were a burden or that disappointment was inevitable because nobody showed up. Over time, working hard and becoming financially independent can turn into more than just a goal. It can become armor, a way to prove you don't need anyone else to survive.

When I started earning enough to feel secure, I found myself pulled toward the idea of escaping the grind. I longed to take a step back, to breathe after pouring so much energy into working and building stability. I needed space to remember who I was outside of all that striving. Traveling became one way to reclaim that space. There's something powerful about arriving in a place where no one knows you, where the noise of daily demands falls away, and you can finally hear yourself again. In that stillness, I reconnected with the parts of me that had been buried under the weight of routine.

Traveling isn't just about seeing new sights or taking pretty pictures. It's about peeling back the layers, sitting with your own thoughts, and feeling what's been waiting for your attention beneath all the busyness. In those quiet moments away from expectations and noise, I started to see that independence for me wasn't really about financial freedom. It was about healing the wounds I carried and rebuilding trust in myself. I needed to learn that I could be safe and whole on my own without having to prove anything to anyone else.

I still remember the moment I realized I needed more than just a quick break, that I needed real time to breathe and readjust my thinking. Work felt endless. My life felt overwhelming. No matter how hard I tried, I couldn't find my footing. I was stuck in a cycle so many of us know too well: push harder, achieve more, stay strong at all costs. Deep down, I was running on fumes. Burnt out and disconnected, I hadn't given myself the time or space to actually look at what I was feeling, let alone begin to heal.

On a whim, I booked a last-minute trip to a small island off the coast of Georgia, a place that had always felt like my secret pocket of peace. I invited my sister to come along. She was pregnant at the time and needed a break just as much as I did. From the moment we arrived, it felt like we both exhaled for the first time in months. We slipped into the island's slow rhythm, lounging by the pool, wandering beneath the sun-soaked, drooping live oak trees, and spending quiet afternoons savoring good food and ocean breeze.

That simplicity reminded me of who I was beneath all the striving. Instead of worrying about what needed to be done next or who I needed to take care of, I was simply there with my sister, present and alive in each moment. I felt something I hadn't felt in a long time: safety inside myself.

On our last evening, we went to one of my favorite restaurants, a little Mexican cabana with a tiki bar right by the water. We sat under a roof of dried palm leaves, soaking in the warm breeze and the sound of waves crashing nearby. I was probably on my tenth piña colada of the weekend, and for once, I wasn't thinking about the emails waiting in my inbox or what tomorrow might bring.

That's when I noticed her, a woman in a bright yellow sundress who walked up to the bar, ordered a strawberry daiquiri, and took a seat alone. She looked completely content, watching the sunset and the waves roll in. The bartender asked if she was waiting on someone and offered her a second menu. She simply smiled and said no before turning back to the ocean, sipping her drink.

I couldn't stop watching her. She wasn't scrolling on her phone, checking her messages, or trying to look busy. She just sat there, fully at ease in her own company. There was no urgency in her posture, no restless shifting, no hunger for distraction. She seemed so at peace, like she had made friends with her own soul.

As I watched her, something clicked inside me. I realized how deeply I craved that kind of calm, that quiet confidence, that solid sense of self that didn't depend on anyone else. I wondered what she had gone through to reach that place. What had she let go of? How had she learned to be so fully present? In that moment, she became a living reminder of what healing could look like for me, not just surviving but actually feeling safe, content, and happy in my own skin.

My mind shifted that weekend. I knew my journey wasn't about escaping or catching my breath for a few days anymore. It was about learning to carry that sense of peace back home with me, to build it inside myself so I wouldn't have to keep running away to find it.

After that trip, I couldn't stop thinking about the woman at the bar. She looked so steady, so anchored in her own presence. I wanted that unwavering peace that lives in your bones. I wanted to reach a place where my happiness came from within, not from constant reassurance or someone standing beside me.

In the weeks that followed, I started to realize that the peace I admired in that woman wasn't just about solitude. It was about self-trust. She seemed like someone who had stopped searching for her reflection in other people, someone who didn't need constant validation to feel steady in who she was. That realization made me look at my own life differently. I began to see how much of my energy had gone into proving my worth through others—through their approval, their affection, their attention. It wasn't just about work anymore; it was about how I showed up in love, too. That quiet strength I longed for wasn't going to come from independence alone but from learning how to belong to myself first.

For most of my life, I thought love meant completely losing myself in another person as proof of my devotion. I believed that if I held on tightly enough, if I molded my life around theirs, it would show how much I cared. But slowly, I learned that needing someone to fill the gaps wasn't love. It was fear. It was a silent plea for someone else to make me feel whole when I hadn't yet learned how to do that on my own. I made a lot of mistakes and lost a lot of relationships because of this.

Healing meant learning to build a foundation within myself first. It meant standing on solid ground even when everything around me felt uncertain. I had to learn that it's OK to lean on others, but it's not their job to keep me upright. I started to understand that true connection is about choosing someone freely, not from a place of survival or desperation but from a place of wholeness. This person needed to be able to walk in and out of my life without causing me to lose my stability. Sure, it could be upsetting and emotional, but I couldn't allow that to shake my basic needs. I had to be the one to supply those things for myself.

When you stop treating relationships as lifelines, they transform. You stop expecting someone else to rescue you from where you live, from loneliness, or from defining your worth. Instead, you invite them into a life that's already rich and alive with your own presence. Love becomes a choice, not a necessity. You can sit across from someone, enjoy their company fully, and still know that your soul is steady whether they stay or go.

That changes everything. It feels lighter, easier, freer. You're able to savor someone's presence and never take it for granted, without also trying to hold them too tightly or fearing they might slip away. You start to respect them as their own person, with dreams, wounds, and needs just like yours. There's space for each of you to grow, to step back when needed, and to move forward together without losing your individual selves.

Choosing companionship over need creates confidence. You begin to see your partner or your friends not as crutches but as fellow travelers, each on their own journey. You can support each other from a place of abundance, not fear or emptiness. You can honor your own rhythms and respect theirs, too. Maybe one of you needs a slow morning alone, while the other loves to jump right into conversation. Maybe one of you feels restored by reading while the other relaxes with gaming or music. There's no pressure anymore to match every single mood and moment.

When you come from a place of stability, you can say yes to love with an open heart instead of an anxious, guarded one. You don't need someone to fix or save you, because you've already learned to give yourself what you need. There's no quiet desperation running beneath the surface, no fear that love might disappear if you stop earning it. Instead, there's a calm steadiness that allows you to meet someone eye to eye. This is where true intimacy is born—in the moments when you both show up as whole people, not halves searching for completion.

From that place, love starts to feel lighter. It isn't tangled with control or performance. It's not built on waiting for a text or trying to guess what the other person is thinking. It's simple, almost quiet, like two steady heartbeats finding rhythm beside each other. The freedom to choose each other every day comes naturally because it feels good to share your life with someone who sees you fully and truly. You stop trying to hold on so tightly, and instead, you let love breathe. It becomes something alive and mutual, grounded in peace rather than fear.

That kind of love feels like home. It's the kind of connection where both people can stand firmly on their own feet yet still choose to reach for each other's hands. The stability comes from knowing they are not there for you out of obligation, and you are not there for them out of need but because you are both choosing, again and again, to love—for no reason other than the simple truth that you want to.

That woman at the tiki bar wasn't sitting there because she had no other option. She was there because she chose her own company first. I wanted to be that person—someone who could love deeply and still hold my own shape, someone who could stand alone and still reach out for connection out of genuine desire.

There was a long time in my life when I didn't understand the difference between being alone and feeling lonely. Loneliness always carried a dull, heavy ache. It was that hollow sense that something or someone was missing, even when I was surrounded by people. I felt it at crowded parties where my laughter wasn't real or in relationships where I felt unseen, no matter how close we were. I thought that if I stayed busy enough, if I kept myself surrounded by noise and company, I could avoid that lonely ache. But no amount of scheduling or background noise ever truly filled it, and I didn't understand why.

It wasn't until I started spending intentional time alone that I realized how different solitude could feel. When I began to slow down and sit with myself, I discovered small joys I had overlooked for years. I loved the way the morning light spilled across the floor when I opened the blinds. I loved listening to the rhythm of my footsteps on a quiet walk instead of filling the silence with music. I loved the smell of coffee brewing while watching the world move outside my window. In those moments, I wasn't missing anyone. I wasn't scanning the room for reassurance or wondering if I was good enough. I was just there, present with myself.

The silence that once felt so threatening began to feel like a friend. Instead of being something to escape, it became a gentle invitation to listen more closely to my own thoughts and pay attention to my emotions. I started to hear myself more clearly, to feel what I had been pushing down beneath all the distractions. Solitude gave me room to understand where my fears were coming from, to recognize the old wounds that had shaped the way I moved through the world. It allowed me to see that so much of my anxiety around connection was really just fear of being alone with myself.

As I learned to enjoy my own company, I noticed I felt more secure in every other part of my life. I wasn't reaching out to people to fill empty spaces anymore. I wasn't bending myself to match what I thought others needed from me. I began to trust that I could give myself the comfort and grounding I had always looked for in others.

Don't get me wrong—this was not an overnight change. It took a lot of patience and practice. There were days when the quiet felt so heavy, when I felt like I needed to be around people again, when old fears rose up, and I felt the urge to distract myself. But over time, those moments became fewer and further between. They became reminders that I was learning to hold space for myself without judgment.

Being alone but not lonely is about coming home to yourself. It's finding joy in your own presence and learning to love the stillness instead of fearing it. It's sitting alone at a restaurant and feeling at ease, or traveling solo and savoring every detail without needing to share it all over social media. When you become your own safe place, solitude stops feeling like something to endure and starts feeling like a breath of fresh air—a place where you can rest, reflect, and reconnect with yourself.

Another common misconception about solitude is that it requires you to close yourself off and push people away. It can feel offensive to some people when you tell them that you'd rather be alone—and that's OK. If someone else chooses to take offense at you needing time to yourself, that has nothing to do with you. It just means they haven't yet figured out how to do that themselves, so they don't understand.

Spending more time alone also taught me how misunderstood solitude can be. People often assume that choosing quiet or space means something is wrong—that you're upset, distant, or pulling away. What they don't realize is that solitude can actually make your relationships healthier. It gives you clarity about what you want to share and what you need to keep sacred. You begin to show up with more honesty and intention because you've reconnected with yourself. That shift naturally carries over into love and partnership, where space stops feeling like disconnection and starts feeling like respect.

In romantic relationships, this means you can make your own choices without needing approval for every little thing. You can enjoy time alone or go out with friends without guilt or fear of upsetting your partner. A healthy relationship respects each person's individuality just as much as the bond you share. Your partner should feel like a safe space, a place where you can land as your full self rather than someone who requires you to give up pieces of who you are.

Friendships follow the same pattern. Real friends don't expect you to perform or always be "on." They understand when you need space or when life demands more of you for a while. Healthy friendships allow for both closeness and independence. You should feel safe showing up exactly as you are. Sometimes you might be radiant, overflowing, and excited, and sometimes you might be quiet and reflective and just want to relax. The best friendships are built on mutual respect and the understanding that love doesn't require constant proximity to be real.

Family dynamics can feel even more challenging. Many people grow up believing that family must always come first and that setting boundaries is selfish or unkind. It's possible to love your family with your whole heart and still honor your own needs. You are allowed to step back when family situations feel overwhelming. You are allowed to protect your peace and your energy and to create space for your own growth, even if others don't fully understand. This might look like staying home for the holidays instead of joining the massive family event that always gives you anxiety, or choosing not to mediate family issues that don't concern you.

Again, choosing to prioritize your well-being does not mean abandoning the people you love. It means ensuring that you can show up for them from a place of wholeness instead of obligation. It might be tempting to go to the family Thanksgiving, where you'll be anxious and miserable the whole time, frustrated with comments being made, sitting in a corner, and not speaking to anyone. But I can almost guarantee that your family would rather you be honest and let them know you need to stay home for the day.

Making these choices will not be simple and will be easier said than done. You might feel guilty. You might feel fear or worry that others will misunderstand why you're choosing to be alone. It's important to remember that your worth is never going to be measured by how much you sacrifice or how constantly available you are to everyone. Your value lies in your ability to live as your true self and to offer love that is genuine and unforced. When you build a life that respects both your independence and your relationships, you create a foundation that supports deeper, more meaningful connections.

If there's one thing I want you to remember, it's this: you are allowed to be your own person. You can protect your peace, honor your needs, and still be loved by everyone around you. The people who truly care about you will understand that choosing rest, quiet, or time alone doesn't mean you care any less. It simply means you are taking responsibility for your own well-being. You don't need to apologize for listening to your body or your emotions when they ask for space. The world will not fall apart because you said no. The people who matter will still be there when you come back, and the time you spend away will help you return with more presence, patience, and warmth. The more you allow yourself these moments of honesty and care, the more fully you'll be able to give and receive love that feels steady, genuine, and alive.

Togetherness is often seen as the ultimate sign of love. We are taught that closeness means commitment, that being inseparable is proof of loyalty, and that distance signals something is wrong. We see it everywhere, in movies, in family traditions, and in the way people speak about devotion as if it requires giving yourself up. These messages run so deep that craving space can feel like betrayal, as if choosing quiet time alone means you are choosing against love itself. The truth is that genuine connection is not measured by how often you are side by side but by how safely you can return to yourself and still feel secure in the bond. Love does not vanish when you step away; it grows stronger when given room to breathe. The more you allow space within togetherness, the more real and balanced that love becomes.

Rewriting these beliefs takes both courage and compassion. It asks you to sit with the discomfort of doing things differently, to challenge the quiet pull that tells you love must always come at your own expense. It's not easy to unlearn the idea that your worth depends on how much you give or how available you are to others. But each time you choose solitude without guilt, you send a new message to yourself and the people around you. You begin to show that love can exist in the same space as independence, that caring for yourself does not compete with caring for others.

Independence also extends far beyond relationships. It's found in the passions and pursuits that light you up, whether that's in your career, your creative work, or your hobbies. When you follow your own interests and dedicate time to things that make you feel alive, you build a sense of self-worth that comes from your own experience and not from someone else's approval. Your career or creative work becomes an extension of who you are and a place where you express your truth and find meaning.

You don't have to share every part of your journey or align your goals with someone else's to feel successful and loved. Creating and exploring for yourself helps you stay grounded and connected to your own life. It's a powerful way to reinforce that you belong to yourself first. True independence is rooted in self-trust. It means knowing who you are and what matters to you, even when no one else is watching. You feel secure enough to make decisions that align with your values, and you understand that your worth is not defined by your relationships, your work, or the roles you play in other people's lives.

Investing in your healing prevents old wounds from spilling into your connections. When you don't value independence and you force yourself to be around people constantly when your pain is still unaddressed, it can cause those relationships to turn sour. It can cause misunderstandings, resentment, or pushing people away before they've had a chance to get close.

Independence can look different for everyone. You might enjoy preparing a meal for yourself. You might take on a project without asking for help, or you might just sit in silence at home and feel completely at ease. You learn to make choices and handle challenges without waiting for assistance or approval. You start to feel confident, knowing that you have the tools to care for yourself emotionally and practically.

You don't need to prove yourself and prove your strength by refusing help at every turn, either.

There is a difference between choosing to be self-reliant and feeling like you have no other option. When independence is driven by fear, it can turn into hyper-independence. You might avoid help because past betrayal taught you that letting others in feels dangerous. You might believe that handling everything on your own is the only way to stay safe.

Hyper-independence often hides in plain sight. On the outside, it can look like strength, confidence, or discipline—the person who has everything handled and never asks for a thing. People might even admire you for it, praising your resilience and work ethic. What they don't see is the constant tension underneath. Every task becomes proof that you can survive without anyone, every success another layer of armor built to protect the parts of you that still remember what it felt like to be let down. It's a quiet exhaustion that never really fades because even rest starts to feel unsafe when you've learned that slowing down might invite disappointment.

You start to mistake isolation for peace. Saying "I've got it" becomes second nature, even when your body is begging for rest or your heart is craving connection. You convince yourself that depending on someone means losing control, that asking for help will only lead to more pain. Over time, you stop realizing how heavy everything has become because you're so used to carrying it alone. That's the trick of hyper-independence—it convinces you that self-protection is freedom, when in truth, it's just another cage built out of fear.

While this protective instinct might have been necessary at one time, over the years it can create isolation and exhaustion. Forcing yourself to carry every burden alone will leave you feeling disconnected and unsupported, even when people around you are willing to help. Accepting support is not a sign of weakness—it's important you remember that. It's simply a way of allowing relief and comfort into your life. When you say yes to help, you are proving your trust and faith in your connections. You do not have to keep fighting every battle alone.

Learning to receive support strengthens your bond with others and offers you the freedom to rest. You learn that you can be strong and open at the same time. Slowly, you realize that support does not threaten your independence—it enriches it. If you notice yourself turning away from help out of fear of being let down, know that you are not alone. Many people feel this way when old wounds still linger close to the surface. Healing these areas takes time and patience. Allowing others in, even in small ways, can bring you unexpected comfort and help soften the walls you have built.

Receiving help can also spark new growth in ways you might not expect. When you finally let others in, the world begins to open up again. You start to see how collaboration can breathe life into your ideas, how a conversation can shift your perspective, or how a small act of kindness can remind you that you're part of something bigger than yourself. Allowing someone to support you doesn't diminish your strength—it expands it. It shows you that connection can be safe, that love can exist without control, and that you can still be independent while letting yourself be cared for.

When you balance independence with openness, your life begins to feel more textured and alive. Creativity flows more freely because you're not spending all your energy holding everything together alone. Relationships start to feel lighter, filled with a sense of reciprocity instead of resistance. You begin to realize that letting someone help you is also a gift to them—an invitation for closeness, trust, and shared humanity. This is where growth becomes less about survival and more about thriving, where healing starts to look like color returning to a world that had gone dim.

Finding independence is a continuous process. It does not have a single moment of arrival but unfolds over time, shaped by the small, consistent choices you make to honor yourself. Each time you choose to trust your needs, listen to your inner voice, and protect your energy, you help build a life that feels steady and true. As you move forward, remember that independence is a daily practice. Some days will feel strong and grounded, and you'll be confident in who you are and how you show up. Other days might feel uncertain, or you might notice old patterns resurfacing. Both sides of the coin are simply part of your growth.

Carrying this sense of self into your relationships allows you to choose connection from a place of freedom. You start sharing your life with others because you genuinely want to, not because you feel incomplete on your own. You're able to give and receive love while holding on to your sense of self.

A foundation of independence also gives you the strength to set boundaries and speak up for your own needs without apology. You'll begin to feel more steady in your decisions and less influenced by what others expect of you. Instead of worrying about keeping everyone happy, you start to trust that staying true to yourself is one of the most loving things you can offer.

As you bring this self-awareness into different parts of your life, you'll begin to notice changes. Your friendships will feel more authentic, your work will feel more aligned, and your sense of purpose will feel stronger.

The goal is never to shut others out or become unapproachable. The goal is to learn that you belong to yourself first. From that place, you can share love and connection in a way that feels open and real. You can hold space for both solitude and closeness.

As you keep going, remember to honor those small moments—the mornings when you feel at ease in your own company, the times when you feel relief instead of guilt, and the moments when you let someone support you without questioning your worth. These are milestones that show you are building a life based on self-respect and inner trust. The more you honor your independence, the more deeply you can engage with the world around you.

You are not here to carry every burden alone, and you do not have to give yourself away to be loved. You are meant to find a balance where you can stand firm in who you are while still allowing space for closeness and care. Love isn't meant to drain you; it's meant to meet you where you already stand whole. You can be soft without losing your strength and open without losing your boundaries. It's the quiet understanding that you can hold your own shape while still reaching for someone's hand, and that you can let people in without disappearing into them.

Chapter 9

Creativity Unleashed

Discovering Power in Self-Expression

As you explore your independence and start giving more of your time to creativity, you'll notice a shift in your grounding. You'll wake up one day and suddenly realize how much inspiration is all around you, in the small and big things. You'll especially notice it when you catch yourself getting so wrapped up in a simple project that you forget to check the clock or when you're so completely focused that the noise of the world just seems to fade into the background.

Those are my favorite moments—the ones where you suddenly look up from whatever you're doing and realize how much time has gone by. In those moments, you're not trying to impress anyone or chase a goal. You don't feel stressed or worried, and you just enter the state of relaxation that you forgot you loved so much. Those moments are so precious and important because you're finally fully present and doing something completely engaged, at peace, and productive.

When you look up and check the clock and realize how much time you've been doing something that makes you feel happy instead of your usual overthinking about your trauma or anxieties about your daily life, it feels amazing. It's your friendly reminder that there's more to life than just pushing forward and checking the boxes.

Now, if you're someone who's considering skipping this chapter because you're convinced that you're not creative and you just don't have the talent to do things like that, I'd urge you to think again. I get it. Maybe you see extra-creative people around you who are constantly making beautiful things, and because you know you don't have the talent they have for those specific tasks, you don't consider yourself a creative person. Or maybe you think that creativity is something people are born with and that creativity belongs to artists, musicians, or people who make a living from making art and are passionate about it.

The truth is, though, that you are far more expressive than you give yourself credit for.

You need to get rid of the narrow definition that's probably floating in your mind that tells you creativity is only doing things like painting, crafting, drawing, or writing. In reality, creativity is so much broader than that, and it lives within almost everything you do—from cooking to arranging flowers in a vase or even how you make your bed. Those are all creative pursuits. It's right there in the word *create*—the dozens of small, everyday choices that make your life feel a little more like yours and a little more personalized are creativity in the works.

Your brain might not be programmed just yet to recognize these moments and these tasks as creative, but they matter just as much as any polished artwork you see from professionals. All these choices are acts of self-expression that bring color and texture to your daily life. They make you feel more at home.

Small choices, like adding a sprinkle of herbs to your meal because it smells good and looks better, or rearranging your furniture for a refreshed feeling and look in your space, are all a part of this natural, personal creativity that you have. It's easy to overlook the small sparks because they seem so mundane, and they're not something you do every day. They don't come with big applause, but they're proof you are capable of being a creative person.

One of the best ways to discover how you can be a creative person is to pay attention to your curiosity and allow yourself some simple experimentation. If you aren't quite sure what lights you up yet, give yourself permission to try activities without expecting yourself to be good at them or expecting them to turn into a beautiful masterpiece. Cook one of those recipes you have saved on your phone that you saw in a video weeks ago—one that you thought sounded good but figured you wouldn't be able to figure out.

Try a dance workout, even if it makes you feel awkward and uncoordinated, or put together an outfit that makes you feel bold and excited to walk out the door. Even small things like doodling on scrap paper while you're waiting on hold on the phone or making a playlist that matches your mood can be super creative and personal to you.

The key is to approach these things with a sense of playfulness and curiosity. Notice what makes you feel relaxed, joyful, or energized, and notice if something makes you feel drained or like you don't want to do it anymore. If you find something that sparks even the tiniest bit of excitement, lean into it. Let yourself explore it freely without needing to justify it or turn it into something serious. You'll probably be surprised by how these small experiments can unlock deeper creativity inside of you.

Once you start noticing these moments, your curiosity will expand, and you'll find yourself wanting to explore more. You'll start toying with the idea that you can be a creative person too. As I said earlier, it's already woven into who you are. We are all born with it—it's just sitting there, waiting for you to pay attention to it and let it be free. The more you allow the small personal touches to surface and become comfortable with them, the more connected and excited you'll feel about the small things. The invitation to create is always there to remind you that there's beauty and meaning hidden in the smallest parts of your day.

One approach to reconnect with your creativity is to think back on what you loved before life became so structured and complicated. Take a moment to think back to your childhood—what activities made you lose track of time? Maybe you were the kid who doodled all over your notebooks, made mud pies and potions in the yard, or spent hours building forts and creating imaginary worlds with your friends or your siblings. A lot of the time, the things we cherished as kids can give us hints about what will bring us joy today.

If you were the kid who doodled all over your notebooks in school, maybe getting a sketchpad or coloring book is what you need in your adult life, even if you haven't done that in years. If you made mud pies and potions in your yard, maybe cooking will inspire you. If you spent hours building forts or creating imaginary worlds, maybe it's video gaming or crafting that you would enjoy today.

If nothing from your past jumps out at you, consider what you enjoy watching or admiring now. Maybe you find yourself binge-watching hours of cooking competitions or home renovation videos, or maybe you find yourself saving photos of gardens, poetry, or even hand-painted signs. Those things that naturally draw your attention, even just as a viewer, can lead you to activities that spark your imagination. When you pay attention to those little nudges of curiosity, they often guide you exactly where you need to go in order to be creative.

One of my personal favorite things to do on a weekend or after a long day at work is to go to my local craft store. I typically don't have anything in particular in mind that I'm looking for—I just aimlessly browse the aisles and let the craft choose me. Sometimes it's paints and a canvas; other times it's diamond art or one of those mini cross-stitching kits. There are dozens of things you can pick up and quickly waste an afternoon doing.

You don't need to feel any kind of pressure to complete or keep whatever it is that you create, either. I've started at least a dozen cross-stitching kits that never ended up seeing the light of day. The point is not to make something perfect. What you're aiming for is the distraction—the journey of doing the thing you decide to purchase and wasting an afternoon or even a weekend on it, allowing it to take you out of your current stressors.

When you let go of plans and procedure and step into creative play, you'll start building trust with your intuition instead of second-guessing each choice. You'll learn to listen to that subtle inner voice, the one that knows what feels right even when you can't explain it. Every decision, whether it's letting the craft at the store pick you, choosing a paint color, or arranging flowers on a table, will become a common practice of checking in with yourself, listening, and following that inner voice to build a stronger connection to your own needs and desires.

Learning to trust your intuition will help you rebuild your self-trust in a way that feels safe and organic. It's normal to have accidentally learned to suppress your instincts to meet outside expectations or even to avoid conflict, but over time, this can create a disconnect from your own desires or feelings. When you give yourself permission to create without rules or expectations, you start to see that your preferences and instincts actually matter. They aren't random. They're meaningful. Every time you follow that small inner nudge, you reconnect with a part of yourself that already knows what feels right, even if you can't fully explain why.

The reason creativity ties into all of this and why it's so healing is that it reminds you to pause and honor your inner world. There's no point in muting your impulses or ideas to keep the peace, to be easy, or to avoid standing out. When you're older, you won't want to look back on your life and wish you could've tried something out, started the company, sold the product, or gotten a booth at the art show. Whatever it is that your mind might be curious about but you've been avoiding, it's not worth the regret.

You hear all the time that you don't want to grow old and regret not doing things when you were younger, but it really is important to value that idea. Creating distance between your comfort levels and your potential will eventually cause you to feel like you're moving forward without purpose, or even worse, staying stagnant. That's exactly what we don't want to do when we're trying to heal ourselves.

Over time, as you form the habit of regularly tuning into your intuition, you'll be laying solid groundwork for your personal growth. There's a well of wisdom within you, always ready to guide you toward whatever feels authentic and nourishing. As long as you keep listening to it and acting on this inner voice, you'll notice your sense of self becoming more robust and grounded. You'll move from seeking validation from the outside world to trusting what's inside of you, and this trust you're building will be incredibly empowering as it grows stronger.

When you practice creating intuitively, it builds confidence in your ability to handle the unknown. You stop feeling like you have to control every detail or predict exactly how things will turn out. Instead, you begin to trust yourself in the process. You learn to move with the experience rather than trying to force the outcome, and that shift makes uncertainty feel far less threatening.

You'll discover that you can handle surprises, things like messing up a painting, adding too much salt to a recipe, or deciding that you don't like how you rearranged your room after all that time you just spent. You'll be able to adapt as necessary and even find joy instead of frustration in those unexpected twists and turns. This mindset shift will extend naturally into other aspects of your life and make it easier to make changes and approach new experiences with curiosity instead of frustration or fear. You'll start to meet your day-to-day life with a soft grip, more willing to just see what happens rather than control every outcome.

Don't get me wrong, creativity will test your patience. Messing up that painting or a recipe or having to undo something you've taken time to create can be really stressful and frustrating. The good news is it will help you build up emotional tolerance at a time when you might already feel on edge every day. The first few times you mess up a project, you might get so frustrated that you want to start over or throw out the craft and try something completely different, and that's okay. You'll get comfortable with it soon enough and be able to just pause and readjust instead of quitting.

On another note, creativity does not always have to be something you do alone. Many people feel really inspired when they're creating alongside others. Sharing ideas, encouraging each other, and just enjoying the process together can bring out a whole new side of expression and inspiration. Maybe you join a dance class, take a pottery workshop, or even start a book club with your friends where you discuss your favorite reads. Even casual small things like cooking for your friends or making a playlist for everyone to listen to on a long drive can be fun, creative expressions.

These are spaces where ideas move freely, where there's conversation and laughter, and where no one is worried about getting it just right. My friends and I have had multiple "craft nights" where we all go to the discount store and pick out four or five silly crafts to do while having some wine. It's in these moments of connection that you uncover new parts of yourself, inspired by the people around you.

It's also just really good to be around people who make you comfortable. Many people hold back from trying new forms of self-expression or creativity because they're worried about looking silly or stepping outside of the box. Fear of judgment and perfectionism can convince you to stay small and avoid taking risks, but underneath that hesitation is often just a need to feel free and to move without self-criticism.

When you're around people who truly support your growth, that fear starts to fade. You don't feel like you have to protect yourself in the same way. Creativity should be a space where you can drop the performance and simply be yourself. It gives you room to release pressure, move stress out of your body, and let your thoughts and emotions flow somewhere safe. In that space, you get to meet a version of yourself that feels honest and unguarded.

Being surrounded by others while you're being creative can also shift how you relate to yourself and how you notice your own tendencies. You might start to see the ways you compare yourself to others or the ways that you hold yourself back by viewing those around you doing the same. Instead of seeing life as a series of competitions or performances, you'll get to see it as a shared journey. You become more willing to share your real thoughts, to ask for help, and to support others without needing to measure your worth against theirs.

If you can't find a group of friends nearby that feels like the right fit for sharing your hobbies, consider starting a group yourself. You might be surprised by how many people are also craving a place to connect and share their interests. Social media, local community boards, or even conversations with peers can help you find others who are looking for the same kind of connection. By taking the time to organize a regular meet-up, whether it's in person, online, or even just starting a group chat, you create a welcoming space where people can gather to share ideas, learn from each other, and offer support. It all begins with you having the courage to reach out and invite others to join you.

You don't have to wait for a perfectly formed group or a big official community to get started. Some of the most meaningful connections happen in small, informal circles that just grow over time. Even if you begin with just one or two people, the shared experience of coming together is what makes it feel special. Your focus when starting a group should not be to build a large following or create a professional environment. It should simply be about genuine exchange, encouragement, and inspiration. You can gather to write, knit, paint, cook, take classes together, or just explore new ideas.

There's warmth in being in a space with others who are also exploring their own creativity. It's really comforting knowing that everyone is showing up with their own mix of doubts, excitement, and things that they're trying to work through in their own lives. You start to realize that the fears you thought were yours alone are actually shared by so many others. This helps you soften the edges of your own self-criticism. You might find yourself feeling braver just by being in the presence of others who are willing to try, and you can even gain a bit of confidence that comes from supporting others in the group.

The energy of a group can push you forward, bring new ideas to life, and remind you that you are not alone. You're not trying to prove anything here, and this only supports the idea that the value isn't in the finished piece but in the act of being seen, creating it, and sharing it with others. You learn to cheer for each small step forward, whether it's yours or someone else's. Vulnerability is not weakness but a strength. Watching someone else light up when they talk about their project can ignite your own excitement, and sharing your struggles might help someone feel less alone. Little by little, you're building the bricks of the foundation of your healing.

It gets easier to let go of embarrassment when you shift your focus from how something looks or how people view it to how it feels inside your body and your mind. Ask yourself honestly, if no one else could see you, what would you feel excited to try? What would you feel curious about? What idea or activity have you held in your heart but avoided because of fear? We often imagine that others are watching and judging us as sharply as we judge ourselves, but quite frankly, people are just absorbed in their own lives. Even if someone does have an opinion at some point, it holds far less weight than your own sense of fulfillment and the peace that comes from doing what feels true to you.

Giving yourself permission to explore freely without the fear of looking silly is you giving yourself self-compassion and confidence. You can start small by yourself in private spaces where you feel comfortable. As I said, the goal is not to produce something impressive but to rediscover the joy of playing. As you feel more at ease, you might choose to share a small piece, like a snippet of writing with a friend or that new dish you cooked for someone you love. You might feel confident enough to go out in an outfit that feels bold and expressive, or in a hairstyle that you wouldn't normally wear. Each small act of sharing and including other people will build your courage and help you move on from the old, rigid boundaries that you once held yourself within for no reason.

Over time, this self-expression will start to feel less like something to hide and be embarrassed about and more like something to celebrate. It becomes a powerful way to reclaim your space in the world and to remind yourself that it is safe to be seen and to be silly. This openness will support your healing and teach you that you can exist fully without shrinking or apologizing. You begin to realize that the world gains more from people who show up as themselves than from those who shrink down and try to blend in. There's no real benefit in making yourself smaller just to fit the space around you.

When you're moving through such a heavy time in your life, making things and being expressive becomes much more than just a fun hobby. It turns into a powerful tool for understanding and releasing your feelings that might otherwise stay trapped inside. Painful experiences often carry emotions that feel really heavy or too complicated to put into words. Expressive activities offer a private and safe way to work through those feelings and let them exist outside of your body and your mind without having to explain them. Instead of feeling swallowed up by your grief or confusion, you can transfer those feelings into something tangible and visible. It can feel like a release and can make them easier to understand and process.

Now, I'm not saying that you need to become the kind of artist that you see online flinging paint wildly across a canvas and screaming, unless of course that genuinely calls to you, no judgment here. Expression looks different for everyone, and there's no single right way to do it. Some people find comfort in bold abstract art with big sweeping strokes, while others feel calm with the quiet focus of a detailed drawing or knitting. Some people might prefer the steady rhythm of journaling, while others find release through playing video games. The most important thing is to discover what feels most natural and true to you and to find the thing that lets you step out of your world.

When you become fully absorbed in a creative space, you can find a rare kind of stillness and peace. Your mind stops spinning in circles about past regrets or future worries and instead sinks into a quiet, almost timeless state. Time seems to stretch, and the outside world fades away. You might not hear the things around you anymore like the TV, chattering, or noisy neighbors. In those moments, there is nothing to prove and no audience to please. It's just you and the connection to what you're making. This kind of focus can be hard to find anywhere else. It transforms your days into a moving meditation and is a gentle way to soothe your spirit and quietly reconnect with yourself.

Another benefit to creativity is that it's a way for you to reclaim your story and step back into that sense of having ownership over your life. Trauma often makes it feel like control has been stolen from you, leaving you with uncertainty and a sense that life is happening to you rather than you living your life. When you're engaging in a project, you get to create the space to decide how you want to hold your memories. You decide how you want to express your emotions, and you decide how you want something to look and how to move forward with it.

This is a declaration of self-trust and independence. It allows you to redefine your relationship with what has happened. You move from feeling powerless to becoming an active participant in your own healing. You shift from carrying pain to finding ways to release it, and when you can't release it, you learn how to hold it with more softness and understanding. It allows you to step forward with a clear sense of who you are and what you want to carry with you into the future. It's not just painting or knitting or whatever it is, it goes so much deeper than that.

Something else that's noteworthy is that creativity allows you to experience natural moments of beginning, finishing, and transition. Just as a project might come to an end or a certain season of growth might naturally close, it's tempting to rush past these moments, always looking for the next thing to do. There's real value in pausing to honor what you've experienced or what you've created and recognizing the time and effort that you've given to it, both in creating the project as well as healing yourself. Both of those things take time and effort, and it's important to honor that. Creating small rituals around transitions can help you mark the shift and give your mind time to understand the change.

This might look like sitting with what you've made for a few minutes, allowing yourself a moment to feel a sense of pride and reflection. It could be journaling about what the experience taught you or how it shaped you. Maybe you take the time to clean the area, get rid of the supplies you didn't use, and frame the artwork or find a way to keep it. It could also be sharing it with others.

However you choose to mark these transitional moments helps you process and release what has passed. This allows you to carry forward the lessons instead of rushing ahead without acknowledgment and moving on to the next thing. Of course, it's always important to keep moving forward, but in the same breath, you need to allow yourself the time to feel proud. Think about ways you can improve and what you might not do next time, just as you learn to heal.

Finding ways to create and express your emotions offers a path forward. It's a way of stepping into a cooler, more empowered version of yourself. When you create something, you prove to yourself that you're capable of bringing something into the world that did not exist before. Whether it's a reframed state of mind or a project, it reminds you that healing is not only about surviving but about shaping what comes next. This is you showing yourself that you are resilient and not someone who will be defined by past events but someone with the power to influence and shape how they will affect you.

There is also a physical benefit to this kind of engagement. Studies have shown that making things and fully immersing yourself in a creative project can help reduce stress and lower cortisol levels. It can even help the brain build new pathways that support emotional resilience. When you are focused on something that feels absorbing, your mind enters a state that is similar to meditation. It activates the brain's reward system and creates a genuine sense of well-being. Even when the activity is small, the impact is real. It gives your body and mind a chance to process things in a healthy and nurturing way.

An honorable mention with creativity, however, is creative blocks. Feeling blocked or stuck is something many people have difficulty with when they're trying to be creative and express themselves. Creative blocks can feel frustrating and discouraging and leave you unsure of where to even begin. If you're in the wrong mindset, they can also reassure you that you aren't a creative person, which is not correct. This could look like you standing in the aisle of a craft store, having no idea what to pick out, or maybe it's staring at the pantry, having no idea what to cook, even though you have loads of ingredients in front of you.

These blocks happen when we spend too much time in our heads, overthinking every step instead of simply moving forward. We worry too much about what to make, how to start, or whether the final result will be good enough. The truth, however, is that the best way to move past this feeling is to stop waiting for the perfect moment and just move forward one foot in front of the other. Action in itself holds power. The choice to start can shift your energy and make it easier to fall into a natural rhythm. You don't have to worry about the next five things; you just have to focus on the very next one right in front of you.

Creative blocks are something that I personally run into with my writing all the time. I have so many thoughts and ideas in my head, and then I sit down in front of my computer to write them all, and suddenly, they're just gone. It's like a magic trick. Once I'm actually there and ready to do it, I'm unmotivated, and I lose my train of thought. I end up scrolling on my phone or distracting myself instead of just starting to type and letting my ideas flow. It's super frustrating, but I've learned firsthand that you can't let it stop you.

You just have to keep going. You don't have to be in love with what you're making, just keep the ball moving, and you can work through the creative block soon enough. Then, in the end, you can go back and make it just how you like it. Typically, once I've dedicated ten or fifteen minutes to just *doing something,* even if I'm not sure how it will turn out and don't know where it's going, my mind tends to get in the right mindset for those ideas to start flowing and for me to move forward with intention.

Another gentle way to move through a creative block is to create small rituals around your practice. This helps take the pressure off and makes things feel like a natural part of your day rather than a big, intimidating task. Set aside a certain time each day or week to focus on doing something creative. Having this consistent window signals to your mind that it's time to explore and play, giving you structure and routine that can make it easier to slip into that mental space. The more you regularly show up, the more natural it begins to feel over time.

Having a dedicated space or a dedicated mood can also break through that feeling of being stuck. It doesn't need to be elaborate. I personally like to light a candle, make a cup of tea, and put on some background music like soft jazz, really low so it's not distracting but enough to take away the dead silence. For you, it might look like having a table by the window where all your tools are always ready for you, and you're able to just open your window, slide into your comfy chair, and get into that headspace.

When you set aside a physical spot just for creating or playing, it becomes easier for your mind to clock in and step into that curious state. It also keeps your creative time from being muddled into other things like work or relaxation. For example, if you try to do a creative project in bed, you might get creative blocks because the bed signals to your brain that it's time to turn off and go to sleep, but here you are trying to be creative. You want to have your own area that has its own energy and feels like an invitation every time you go near it.

Of course, sensory cues can always help guide you into an open mindset. Music, which is something that I use, is always a great tool. A certain playlist can become a signal that it's time to start. Scents work beautifully too, like lighting a candle or having an essential oil diffuser, or maybe even fabrics like a cozy blanket. You can get creative with the ritual. The goal is to figure out what makes you shift into that mindset and stick with it.

The more you build these small creative rituals, the more you'll start to notice how they shift your attention away from constant consumption and back toward creation. It's easy to fall into the habit of filling every quiet moment with noise—scrolling, watching, or listening to something new—but rituals remind you that silence and stillness are where ideas often take shape. They help you slow down long enough to notice your own thoughts instead of absorbing everyone else's. That's where creativity begins to thrive, in the space between taking things in and allowing something original to come out.

These days, it's incredibly easy to spend hours consuming content. Social media, podcasts, books, videos. There's always something new pulling at your attention. A lot of it can be helpful or inspiring. The problem is when you stay in consumption mode all the time. After a while, it can blur your own thoughts and leave you feeling disconnected from what you actually think or feel. If you notice that happening, try balancing what you take in with something you create. Even small acts of creativity help you hear your own voice again and build a life that feels more personal and grounded.

Creativity offers that space for you to move from being a passive observer, consuming everything, to being an active participant in your own life. This balance doesn't require you to give up consuming altogether. I think it's safe to say that we all have the guilty pleasure of mindlessly doom-scrolling on our phones or binge-watching TV shows. It's also where you can get the spark for powerful new ideas. The key is just to notice when you are using consumption to avoid your own work or to silence your own creative urges. Check in regularly with yourself and learn to recognize when it's time to pause, stop consuming, and do something instead.

In the end, self-expression and healing are closely tied. Both call for vulnerability, change, and growth. Both remind us that we have the power to create something new out of something that once felt broken or lost or something that didn't even exist. No matter where you are on your path, remember that this way of connecting to yourself is always within reach. It's waiting to bring warmth and life even into the darkest corners. All I ask of you is to find the courage to take that first step.

Chapter 10

Love's Invitation

Reopening Your Heart

After trauma, the experience of love often feels inaccessible. It does not disappear in an obvious or dramatic way; it becomes overshadowed. Other emotions take priority because they feel more urgent and more protective. Anger, resentment, fear, and emotional numbness tend to surface quickly. They are sharper and louder, and they demand attention in a way love does not. When the nervous system perceives threat or injury, it shifts its focus toward survival, and connection gets put on the back burner.

This shift is rarely conscious. Most people do not sit down and decide to close their heart; the body does it on its own. It tightens and becomes alert to subtle changes in tone, expression, and proximity. It scans for cues that something could go wrong. Situations that once felt neutral may begin to feel loaded. The system becomes cautious around closeness, especially if closeness was involved in the original wound. Guardedness begins to feel intelligent, and distance begins to feel responsible.

Anger often takes center stage during this phase. After chaos, it can feel steadying. It helps make sense of what happened. It names the wrongdoing and draws a clear line between what was acceptable and what was not. In many cases, anger feels more stable than grief. Grief leaves you exposed to longing, while anger restores a sense of strength. There is a structure to anger that can make it feel safer to live in, especially when everything else has felt uncertain.

Resentment often follows close behind. It begins to shape how you see things. It narrows interpretation and reduces ambiguity. When something has felt deeply unfair, resentment can feel justified because it carries a sense of moral clarity. For some, it becomes woven into identity. The story of what happened turns into a reference point, and the emotional tone attached to it starts influencing how new experiences are understood.

There is often an unspoken belief underneath this protective posture: if I soften, I will be hurt again. If I let go of this anger, then what happened to me loses significance. If I open myself, I am inviting risk. These thoughts may not be articulated clearly, but they influence behavior, tone, and how much of oneself is offered in relationships.

Over time, this protective state can start to feel normal. Vigilance becomes your baseline, and emotional restraint turns into habit. You may notice that you share less than you used to or hold back affection without fully meaning to. Conversations stay surface-level even when part of you wants something deeper. When someone expresses care, there can be a slight pause inside you. The body tightens before the mind has time to explain it.

The difficulty is that protection does not sort carefully between real danger and present safety. Once your system has learned that closeness can lead to harm, it can begin treating all closeness as a potential threat. Love becomes linked with exposure, exposure with vulnerability, and vulnerability with pain. After a while, those links feel automatic, even when the situation in front of you is different from the one that hurt you.

It is also possible that a part of you prefers the guarded version of yourself. Being closed can feel structured, predictable, and less emotionally volatile. When the range of feeling narrows, there is less unpredictability. You may not feel as much joy, but you also do not feel as much risk. That trade-off can seem reasonable, especially in the early stages of healing.

At some point, though, the cost starts to show. Moments that should feel warm land flat. Interactions that used to feel easy begin to require more effort. Suspicion can surface in places where trust once felt automatic. You may tell yourself that you are just being wiser now, more realistic, more careful. There may be truth in that. Trauma does sharpen discernment. The problem begins when discernment slowly turns into distance that never relaxes.

Closing your heart was not weakness; it was a protective adaptation. It reduced overwhelm and created stability during instability. It served a purpose. The question is not whether the closure made sense at the time, but whether it is still necessary at its current intensity.

Before attempting to reopen your heart, it is important to understand the function it has been serving. It has been trying to prevent further injury, preserve dignity, and maintain control in situations where control once felt lost. Approaching this process without acknowledging that function can create internal resistance.

Reopening your heart requires more than deciding to feel differently. It requires recognizing that your system has been operating under the assumption that openness equals risk. Until that assumption is examined, any attempt to feel love again will feel forced or artificial.

Understanding why your heart closed is the beginning of reopening it, not with pressure or urgency, but with clarity. Once you understand that your heart closed for protection, the next question naturally follows: what happened to the love that once felt accessible?

In most cases, it did not disappear. It became inaccessible because it was buried beneath stronger survival responses. Love is not an emergency emotion. It does not override fear or anger when the system is on alert. Instead, it becomes quiet when protection becomes loud.

When trauma occurs, the body shifts its focus to safety. Energy moves toward monitoring, bracing, and anticipating what might go wrong. That shift changes how love is felt. You may still care about people and still want connection, yet the physical sense of warmth, openness, or ease can be harder to reach. It can feel as if something inside you has gone quiet or offline.

Part of this response is physiological. Trauma affects the nervous system. When the body remains guarded for a long time, it does not move easily between activation and rest. It stays prepared. Muscles hold subtle tension. Breathing becomes shallow without you realizing it. Your chest may feel tight, and your stomach unsettled. In that state, emotions tied to safety and connection have difficulty surfacing because the body does not yet recognize that it is safe.

Love is not only an idea; it is also a bodily experience. It is felt in relaxed breathing, lowered shoulders, steady eye contact, and the absence of bracing. When those physical states are restricted, love feels restricted. This can create the illusion that it is gone.

There is also a cognitive layer to this. After being hurt, the mind adjusts its expectations. It becomes more cautious about trust and quicker to anticipate disappointment. It causes you to go into situations expecting a disappointing outcome, this way you are not surprised or hurt again when it is. Neutral behavior can start to feel like a potential threat. These reactions are not signs of cynicism; they are attempts to predict and prevent future pain. The brain is trying to protect you from experiencing the same hurt again.

Because of this, love may begin to feel distant—not because it is gone, but because you cannot fully relax into it. You may still show up for people and continue to care. You may still act with kindness. Yet internally, something feels held back. Spontaneity decreases. Surrender feels risky. Emotional vulnerability requires more effort.

It is important to distinguish between absence and inhibition. Love can be inhibited without being absent. It can be present but compressed, present but guarded, present but waiting for conditions that feel safer.

You may even catch small glimpses of it. A brief warmth when someone speaks gently. A quiet ache when you see something beautiful. A moment of softness that surprises you and then quickly retreats. These moments are often dismissed because they feel inconsistent. Yet they are evidence that love remains accessible beneath the layers of protection.

The difficulty is that accessing love again requires lowering the intensity of the protective state. That shift does not happen through force; it happens through safety. The body needs repeated experiences of consistency, stability, and predictability before it begins to loosen its grip.

This is why telling yourself to simply feel love again rarely works. Love does not respond to pressure; it responds to safety. As safety increases, even gradually, love becomes easier to recognize and feel.

Understanding that love has not disappeared but has instead been inhibited changes the approach. The task is not to create a new emotion. It is to slowly reduce the barriers that have been keeping it contained.

From here, the focus turns to the body, because that is where much of the inhibition resides.

If love feels inhibited, the next place to look is not the mind but the body. Trauma is not stored as narrative alone; it is stored as sensation. The body remembers tone, proximity, pressure, absence, and unpredictability. It records what felt overwhelming and what felt unsafe. Even when conscious memory fades or becomes less vivid, the physical imprint can remain active.

You may notice this in ways that feel subtle but persistent: a tightness across your chest with no clear medical cause, a jaw that stays clenched without intention, shoulders that rarely fully drop, or constant low-level fatigue that is difficult to explain. These are not dramatic symptoms. They are often quiet and steady, becoming so familiar that you forget they were not always present.

When the body remains in a guarded posture, it does not fully enter states associated with connection. Safety is a prerequisite for openness. If your nervous system continues to interpret the world as unpredictable, it will not relax into vulnerability. This does not mean you are unwilling; it means your system is prioritizing protection.

Breathing patterns often reveal this first. After trauma, breathing can become shallow or restricted without conscious awareness. The breath stays higher in the chest, exhalations shorten, and the body remains slightly braced, as if preparing to respond. In that state, emotions connected to warmth and ease struggle to surface fully. The body cannot register enough safety to experience them without restraint.

The same is true of muscle tension. The body may hold contraction in specific areas—neck, shoulders, stomach, and hips. These contractions are not random; they are protective patterns. Muscles tighten to guard vital areas, and over time those patterns can become habitual. You may believe you are relaxed while still holding significant tension.

Reopening the heart requires addressing this physical holding, not through dramatic interventions but through attention. The first step is noticing. Where do you brace when someone moves closer? Where does your body tighten when a conversation becomes emotional? Do you withdraw physically before you withdraw verbally? These reactions often occur before conscious thought.

There can also be a reflexive withdrawal in response to eye contact, tone, or touch. You may feel your body subtly pull back even while your words say that you are fine. That reaction is not hypocrisy; it is protection moving faster than conscious thought.

Rather than trying to override these responses, the work is to notice them without judgment. When your chest tightens, acknowledge it. When your stomach drops, name it quietly to yourself. When your breathing shortens, pay attention to it. The goal is not to force relaxation but to recognize the pattern. Awareness helps reduce automatic reactions.

Gradual regulation begins with small, controlled experiences of safety. You might slow your exhale so it extends slightly longer than your inhale. You might let your shoulders drop and observe whether they lift again. You might sit with a sensation instead of distracting yourself from it immediately. These actions retrain the nervous system to tolerate calm without expecting harm.

It is also important to understand that the body may resist this shift at first. Relaxation can feel unfamiliar. For some people, calm feels more threatening than tension because tension has been consistent. When the body starts to soften, a brief sense of vulnerability may surface. That response does not mean you are regressing; it means your system is adjusting.

Over time, as the body experiences repeated moments of safety without negative consequence, the intensity of the guard can lessen. Muscles begin to release more quickly, breathing deepens without effort, and the chest feels less compressed. In those moments, even brief ones, emotional range begins to widen. Warmth becomes easier to access, empathy feels less risky, and closeness feels less destabilizing.

The body has to learn that it no longer needs to maintain a constant and high level of defense. As physical contraction reduces, emotional availability increases. Love becomes easier to feel because there is finally space for it to surface.

From there, the next step is carefully reintroducing safe forms of connection so that the body can associate closeness with stability rather than threat.

Once the body begins to soften, even slightly, the next phase is not immediate immersion back into intense human connection. That would overwhelm the system. The nervous system relearns safety gradually and needs experiences of connection that feel predictable, contained, and non-demanding. This is where low-risk forms of love become important.

For many people, the first return to felt safety does not happen through romantic relationships or emotionally vulnerable conversations. It often begins in environments or with beings that do not require performance. Animals are one of the most accessible bridges. Their presence does not demand explanation, question your emotional state, or require you to be fully expressive. A dog resting beside you or a cat settling into your lap does not ask for your history. The interaction is simple and direct, and the nervous system can begin to register that steadiness.

That predictability matters. When an animal responds with the same tone, the same physical cues, and the same approach over time, the body starts to relax. There is no sudden change in loyalty and no hidden meaning to decode. That consistency allows the nervous system to recalibrate what closeness can feel like. Proximity begins to register as calm rather than as threat.

Nature works in a similar way. The ocean does not adjust its rhythm based on your mood. The wind does not withdraw if you are guarded, and sunlight does not evaluate you before it warms your skin. These experiences may seem simple, but they communicate reliability. The nervous system responds to patterns, and when those patterns remain steady, internal vigilance can soften.

Spending time in natural settings can also reduce the sensory overload that often follows trauma. Artificial lighting, noise, crowded spaces, and constant digital input can keep the body subtly activated. In contrast, repetitive natural patterns—waves breaking, leaves moving, steady wind—create rhythm. Rhythm stabilizes the nervous system, and that stabilization makes emotional openness easier to tolerate.

This does not mean that sitting outside once will restore emotional capacity. The process is cumulative. Repeated exposure to safe environments gradually shifts baseline tension. The body begins to experience longer stretches without bracing, and that extended calm allows emotional range to widen.

Small acts of kindness function as another controlled reintroduction to love. They are intentional but contained. Holding a door, complimenting a stranger, buying the person's coffee behind you in line, responding thoughtfully to a message, or checking on someone briefly without overextending yourself are manageable risks. They allow you to participate in connection without surrendering entirely. They also reestablish agency. Trauma often disrupts a sense of control, and choosing to act with care reintroduces measured engagement.

It is important to distinguish between performative kindness and regulated kindness. Performative kindness is driven by a need for approval or validation. Regulated kindness is steady and measured; it stays within your capacity and does not leave you depleted. When kindness comes from a stable internal place, the body begins to associate giving with safety rather than with self-abandonment.

You may notice that even small gestures create internal shifts. Your chest might feel slightly less tight after a genuine exchange. You may sense a brief warmth that you would have dismissed months earlier. These changes are subtle and easy to overlook, yet they suggest that emotional responsiveness has not disappeared. It is returning gradually.

Resistance is also common at this stage. Part of you may question whether these small steps make any difference. You may feel impatient and want a noticeable emotional shift instead of gradual recalibration. That impatience is understandable. However, trying to rush the process often reactivates the same protection you are attempting to soften.

Low-risk expressions of love rebuild capacity without overwhelming it. The goal is not intensity but consistency. The nervous system learns through repetition rather than dramatic change. Each steady interaction becomes information, and each calm exchange becomes evidence that closeness does not always lead to harm. An easy goal to manage this is to tell yourself to do two acts of kindness per week. This way, you're remaining consistent while not asking too much of yourself at once.

Over time, these experiences accumulate. You may find that you can tolerate eye contact longer without discomfort. You may notice that you do not immediately withdraw or redirect when someone expresses appreciation. You may feel less internal resistance to shared space. These shifts are physiological and emotional recalibrations occurring in tandem.

As safety increases in controlled environments, the system becomes more open to expanding that safety into more complex human relationships. The foundation must be steady before it is stretched. Without this gradual phase, attempts at deep reconnection can feel destabilizing.

Reopening the heart is about retraining the body to recognize safety in closeness again. Animals, time in nature, and small acts of regulated kindness create contained spaces where that retraining can happen without overwhelming your system.

From there, the focus gradually returns to human trust, which carries more complexity and requires more intention.

As safety becomes more consistent in low-risk settings, the question of human connection naturally resurfaces. This is often where the process feels more complicated. Trusting people involves more unpredictability than trusting nature or animals. Human relationships include interpretation, shared history, shifts in tone, unmet expectations, and the possibility of misunderstanding. For someone who has been hurt, those variables can feel destabilizing.

Rebuilding trust does not start with blind faith. It begins with controlled exposure to reliability. The nervous system responds to patterns, not promises. When someone shows up consistently, follows through on small commitments, and maintains steady behavior over time, your body begins to register that consistency as evidence. Repeated reliability builds trust more effectively than reassurance alone. I wouldn't recommend that you suddenly decide to trust someone with reopening your heart when that person has repeatedly let you down in the past. Find the person who has shown you consistency with their actions day after day, no matter what.

It is important to allow this process to unfold gradually. After trauma, there is often a tendency toward one of two extremes: complete withdrawal or rapid overexposure. Withdrawal keeps you isolated, while overexposure overwhelms the system and can reinforce fear if the interaction does not go well. Sustainable reconnection sits between those extremes. It involves measured steps that increase vulnerability in increments rather than leaps.

You might begin by allowing conversations to last a little longer before retreating into distraction. You might practice expressing a small preference instead of automatically accommodating someone else. You might accept help with something minor rather than insisting on total independence. These moments challenge the internal belief that connection is dangerous.

Alongside these actions, an internal recalibration is taking place. When someone treats you with care, your body may respond with suspicion at first. That reaction does not mean the care is insincere; it means your system has not yet updated its expectations. Instead of dismissing kindness immediately, it can help to pause and notice the discomfort. Where does it show up physically? Does your chest tighten? Does your stomach clench? Do you scoff and make a scrunched-up face instead of smiling and accepting it? Awareness interrupts automatic withdrawal.

Rebuilding trust also requires tolerating uncertainty. No relationship can guarantee permanent safety. After betrayal or loss, that reality can feel intolerable. The impulse may be to look for absolute certainty before opening up again. Absolute certainty does not exist in human connection. What does exist is discernment. Discernment develops by observing patterns over time rather than reacting to isolated moments.

Part of reopening the heart involves separating past threat from present interaction. Trauma compresses time. A current disagreement can trigger the emotional intensity of a previous rupture. Learning to pause and evaluate whether the present situation truly reflects the past is essential. This is not about ignoring red flags; it is about making sure that old wounds are not automatically deciding what happens next.

Grief can also surface at this stage. As you begin to trust again, you may become more aware of what was lost and how much of yourself you had shut down. That realization can be uncomfortable. It can bring forward sadness that had been pushed aside. Reopening the heart does not only restore positive emotion; it restores range. That range includes vulnerability to disappointment, but it also makes room for genuine closeness.

Boundaries become especially important here. Trust is not the absence of limits; it is the presence of clear ones. When you communicate what is acceptable and what is not, you create a structure that makes openness safer. Boundaries are not walls; they are parameters. They allow connection without self-abandonment. When boundaries are respected, trust strengthens. When they are crossed, you gain information.

Over time, reliable interactions accumulate. The body learns that not every closeness ends in harm, and the mind begins to update its expectations. Reflexive bracing softens. You may notice that you do not jump to worst-case scenarios as quickly, that you feel less urgency to withdraw at the first sign of discomfort, and that you can tolerate emotional depth without feeling destabilized.

Trust is rebuilt in pieces. Each small experience of safety contributes to a larger internal shift. As those experiences build on one another, the heart becomes less guarded by default. Openness starts to feel less like risk and more like choice. That distinction matters. When openness is a choice rather than a compulsion, love can exist alongside discernment instead of replacing it.

From here, the focus turns toward how love remains sustainable—how to keep the heart open without losing stability or self-respect.

As trust begins to rebuild, another challenge often appears. Opening your heart again can slowly turn into overextending yourself if you are not paying attention. After trauma—especially trauma involving rejection, abandonment, or betrayal—there can be a quiet urgency to secure connection. You may feel pressure to prove that you are easy to love, agreeable, accommodating, or undemanding. That impulse can look like openness, but it is often anxiety beneath the surface.

Reopening your heart does not mean returning to the version of yourself that tolerated harm. It does not require self-sacrifice. Sustainable love depends on the opposite. Without structure, openness becomes vulnerability without protection, and that imbalance eventually creates instability again.

Boundaries are not emotional distance; they are clarity. They mark where you end and another person begins. After trauma, particularly relational trauma, those lines can blur. You may have learned to override discomfort in order to preserve connection. You may have dismissed early warning signs because you wanted stability more than you wanted truth. Reopening the heart requires correcting that pattern.

Boundaries begin internally before they are spoken aloud. They involve noticing what drains you, what unsettles you, and what consistently leaves you tense afterward. These signals are often subtle at first. You may feel mild irritation, lingering fatigue after certain conversations, or a slight tightening in your chest when something crosses a line. If those cues are ignored repeatedly, they grow louder. The body rarely whispers twice.

Learning to respect those internal signals rebuilds self-trust. When you acknowledge discomfort instead of explaining it away, you reinforce that your experience matters. That reinforcement strengthens stability. Stability, in turn, allows openness without the fear of losing yourself inside someone else's needs.

It is also important to understand that saying no does not close the heart; it protects it. Many people equate love with unlimited availability, and that belief often leads to resentment. Love that endures is structured. It contains mutual respect, allows disagreement, and tolerates individuality. When boundaries are present, connection becomes more secure because both people understand the parameters.

There may be discomfort in asserting limits, particularly if you fear rejection. Early boundary-setting can trigger anxiety. You may anticipate conflict or worry that you will be perceived as difficult. That reaction is common, especially if previous experiences taught you that boundaries lead to punishment or withdrawal. Practicing limits in low-stakes situations can help recalibrate this fear. Each time a boundary is respected, the nervous system updates its expectations.

Boundaries also prevent reenactment. Without them, unresolved trauma patterns tend to repeat. You may find yourself drawn to familiar dynamics simply because they feel recognizable, even when they are unhealthy. Clear limits interrupt that cycle. They slow the pace of attachment and create space for reflection instead of impulse.

Loving yourself at this stage requires consistency. It means checking whether your behavior matches your internal experience. If you feel overwhelmed but continue agreeing to more, there is a disconnect. If you feel dismissed but stay silent to preserve harmony, there is a disconnect. Correcting those misalignments strengthens integrity, and integrity stabilizes the heart.

As boundaries become stronger, something shifts. Openness no longer feels reckless; it feels deliberate. You are not abandoning caution; you are integrating it. Love becomes less about intensity and more about steadiness. It becomes something you engage in consciously rather than something you fall into without structure.

When the heart reopens with boundaries in place, connection becomes more durable. You can care deeply without losing yourself in someone else. You can give without depletion and receive without guilt. Love becomes sustainable because it rests on self-respect.

From here, the final stage involves recognizing that love does not exist in isolation. It exists within networks of connection that support growth and stability over time.

As your capacity for trust strengthens and your boundaries become clearer, love begins to take on a different shape. It no longer feels like a single emotion you either possess or lack. Instead, it becomes relational. It moves between you and the world in steady exchanges rather than dramatic declarations.

Healing is rarely sustained in isolation. Even if much of the internal work happens alone, long-term stability depends on connection—not in the sense of constant interaction, but in the sense of being seen accurately and responded to consistently. When you begin choosing relationships intentionally rather than out of habit or fear of being alone, the quality of your environment changes.

You may begin to notice who feels regulating to be around. Certain people leave your nervous system more settled than activated. Conversations with them do not require performance. You do not rehearse your words before speaking or scan for hidden criticism. You can disagree without fearing abandonment. These may not seem like dramatic signs, but they matter. They signal relational safety.

Other connections may feel energizing but destabilizing. Intensity can be mistaken for closeness, and familiar chaos can be mistaken for chemistry. Part of reopening the heart involves learning to recognize the difference. Love that supports healing does not keep you in a constant state of emotional volatility. It allows steadiness.

Over time, the relationships you choose and nurture begin to form a network—not necessarily a large one, but a reliable one. A friend who listens without correcting you. A partner who remains consistent in tone and behavior. A family member who respects your limits. A therapist, mentor, or community space that offers steady support. These connections create reinforcement. If one interaction is difficult, the entire structure does not collapse because stability exists in more than one place.

Being part of a healthy network also requires reciprocity. Love is not sustained by one-sided effort. When you are regulated and self-aware, you can offer the same steadiness that you value in others. You respond rather than react, repair rather than withdraw, and communicate rather than assume. Over time, that mutual reinforcement strengthens trust.

There is also a subtle shift in identity that occurs here. Instead of defining yourself by what hurt you, you begin defining yourself by how you participate in connection now. Trauma may always be part of your history, but it does not have to dictate your relational posture indefinitely. The heart that once closed for protection becomes capable of measured openness without losing discernment.

This stage does not eliminate vulnerability. Disappointment, conflict, and loss remain possible. Reopening the heart does not remove risk from human experience; it increases resilience in the presence of risk. You are no longer operating from reflexive defense but from informed choice.

In this sense, love is not something you chase or try to create on demand. It grows out of the structure you have built—a regulated body, intentional trust, clear boundaries, and chosen connection. When those elements are in place, love feels less like a surge and more like a steady current. It shows up in conversations, shared silence, ordinary routines, and quiet moments of understanding.

You may not have one dramatic realization that your heart is open again. The change is usually gradual. You might notice that you do not brace as quickly, that kindness no longer feels suspicious and uncomfortable, and that you can care about someone without immediately fearing loss.

Reopening your heart is not about returning to who you were before trauma. It is about integrating what you have learned without letting it harden you. Protection served its purpose. It does not need to define how you move forward. When safety, discernment, and connection exist together, love becomes sustainable.

At that point, love is no longer something you are trying to recover. It is something you are actively participating in again.

Chapter 11

Self-Love Unlocked

Aligning Mind, Body and Heart

So, you've built your networks of love, nurtured them, and spread them out, creating a circle of positivity and support around you. But there's one crucial network you might have overlooked—the one with yourself. It's easy to focus on the love and support you give and receive from others, but remember, the most important connection you can nurture is the one you have with yourself. How can you expect to fully embrace the love from others if you don't first offer that same love and care to yourself? It's time to expand your circle, and this time, make sure it includes the most important person: you.

Take a moment to pause and really look at yourself. Think about the seasons of your life, the ways you've changed, and all the versions of you that have come and gone. You've adapted to new environments, built new routines, and started over more times than you probably remember. You've faced situations that required strength you didn't think you had and kept going even when you felt unsure. Life has been a constant process of growth and readjustment, of finding balance in the middle of change. Through it all, your mind and body have been your constants. They've carried you through every stage, every transition, and every recovery. No matter what you've been through, they have stayed with you.

Your body has been your home through every experience. It has held your joy, your sorrow, your excitement, and your exhaustion. It's carried the weight of your emotions, processed your pain, and found ways to keep you standing even when you were tired or hurting. Think about all the miles it has walked, the nights it has healed while you slept, the moments it has held you together when everything felt uncertain. Your body has always been there, doing its best to protect and support you, even when you didn't always treat it with the same care. It deserves your gratitude and your respect in this very moment.

It's important to love your body exactly as it is right now. It doesn't need to be smaller, bigger, leaner, or smoother to be worthy of love. It has already proven its worth by simply carrying you this far. The lines, scars, and curves all tell your story. They are evidence of endurance, of movement, of life. When you begin to see your body not as something to change but as something to thank, you release the weight of judgment. You start to find peace in simply existing as you are, without needing to become anything else.

Your body has been your most loyal companion. It has weathered illness, heartbreak, fear, and fatigue without ever giving up on you. Think about that kind of loyalty. Think about what it means to have something that never leaves your side. You wouldn't criticize or neglect a friend who's been that faithful to you. You would care for them, thank them, and remind them how much they matter. Your body deserves the same tenderness. It doesn't need to earn your love through change or achievement. It simply needs to be seen and cared for.

When you start treating your body like a friend instead of a project, everything changes. You stop measuring your worth by what you see in the mirror and start measuring it by how you feel when you're gentle with yourself. Each act of care—resting, feeding yourself healthy foods, exercising, speaking kindly, slowing down—becomes a way of saying, "I'm here for you." That is what it means to truly love yourself. It is not about perfecting your reflection but about honoring the partnership that has carried you through every part of your life.

Imagine having a friend who is always there for you. Someone who listens without judgment, who comforts you when you're hurting, and who never walks away, no matter what you're going through. You would never speak to that person with cruelty. You would never shame them for how they look or how long it takes them to heal. You would treat them with patience, gentleness, and care. That same level of compassion is what your body deserves from you. It has carried you through every difficult day, every sleepless night, every moment of worry and joy. It shows up for you without question, no matter how much pressure you put on it. Your body has been your most faithful companion, and it deserves to be treated with the same respect you give to the people you love most.

Setting goals for your body is healthy when those goals come from a place of care, not comparison. The moment you try to change yourself just to look better or to fit into someone else's definition of beauty, you lose connection with your own truth. Your body is not a problem to solve or an image to perfect. It's your home for this life. You don't need to hide it or reshape it to be accepted. It doesn't exist to please the world around you. It exists to hold you, to move you, and to let you experience everything life has to offer. When you stop treating your body like a project and start seeing it as something sacred, you begin to understand what true self-love really means.

There's a real difference between changing your body to look better and caring for it so you can feel better. One is driven by pressure and fear, while the other grows from love and respect. You can eat well, move more, or set health goals—but let them come from the desire to feel strong, clear, and alive. It's important to take care of your body from a place of respect and not a place of insecurity. Let your goals be about how you experience your days, not about how you appear in them. When your choices come from love instead of judgment, the changes you make become sustainable. They're no longer about chasing perfection but about nurturing peace within yourself. True transformation starts when you realize your worth doesn't increase with appearance—it grows through how you care for yourself.

Confidence is rooted in the mind, not the body. I can promise you that no matter how much weight you lose, how many scars you cover, or how many changes you make—whether through surgery or a new wardrobe—there will always be something you find to criticize about yourself. True confidence comes from within, and it's about learning to embrace who you are right now, as you are. The real work begins when you cultivate that inner confidence, regardless of external factors, and then set your health goals from a place of self-assurance.

When you approach your goals with confidence already in place, you are far more likely to succeed. This mindset shifts your focus from striving for perfection to honoring your body and your journey. By building confidence first, you're setting yourself up for a healthier, more sustainable path forward. You'll be able to trust yourself, support your decisions, and face challenges with the resilience needed to continue growing. Confidence isn't about fixing flaws; it's about accepting yourself fully, as you are, and creating a space where health goals become an expression of love and care for your body, not a means of seeking approval.

Paying attention to how you feel is one of the most essential practices you can adopt for your overall health and well-being. Every day, your body sends you signals—whether through physical sensations, emotional shifts, or even changes in your energy levels. Being in tune with these messages allows you to identify what works for you and what doesn't. It's easy to overlook subtle signs, but when you start to pay closer attention to how your body reacts to different foods, activities, or stressors, you can make more informed decisions about your health. This awareness is the foundation for healing, as it empowers you to align your actions with what your body truly needs.

One important aspect of this journey is researching and trying different things to see what resonates with you. There's no one-size-fits-all approach when it comes to health, and what works for someone else might not be right for you. This is why exploring various diets, exercise routines, or mental wellness practices can be so valuable. Whether you're testing out a new eating plan, experimenting with a workout that feels good, or even diving into mindfulness techniques, each new experience adds a layer of knowledge that helps you better understand your unique needs. It's about finding the right fit for your body and mind, allowing you to nurture both in a way that supports your healing.

Embarking on your own health journey is a personal and empowering process. While advice from others is valuable, there comes a time when you must take ownership of your own healing path. It's crucial to recognize that healing isn't linear and that everyone's journey is different. Just because someone swears by a specific routine because it worked out so well for them does not mean you will get the same results if you follow that same routine. The key is being patient with yourself and remaining open to trying new approaches. By taking the initiative to explore what works best for you, you begin to take control of your own well-being. It's your body, your life, and your journey—and only you can determine what will bring you the most healing and fulfillment.

In the process of healing, both mentally and physically, this sense of autonomy helps you align your clarity. When you consciously choose what nourishes your body and supports your mind, you create a harmony between the two. You begin to experience mental clarity that allows you to approach challenges with a fresh perspective. Physical changes can also promote a sense of mental sharpness, as taking care of your body often leads to improved mood, reduced stress, and better cognitive function. This alignment between the mind and body is a powerful catalyst for healing, as it sets the stage for long-term well-being and growth.

Ultimately, your body is your personal home, and it's essential to equip it with the right tools to succeed in healing. Just as you would take care of a home by maintaining its structure and providing for its needs, you must do the same for your body. This means providing the proper nutrients, movement, rest, and self-care to support your healing process. By being proactive in exploring what works best for you, you are giving your body the foundation it needs to thrive. When you treat your body with the care and respect it deserves, it becomes a powerful ally in your journey toward healing, strength, and overall well-being.

At the heart of all these practices—paying attention to how you feel, trying different approaches to health, and aligning your body and mind—is self-love. When you take the time to truly listen to your body, research what helps you feel your best, and give yourself the care and attention you deserve, you are actively showing love to yourself. Self-love isn't just about feeling good in the moment, it's about making the commitment to your own well-being. By honoring your body's signals and giving it the tools it needs to heal and thrive, you send a powerful message that *you are worthy of that attention and care*. It's in these small, everyday choices that self-love becomes a foundational part of your journey.

Building love for yourself also means stepping into your own power. As you explore what works best for you and create a health plan that aligns with your body's needs, you are taking ownership of your life and your healing process. This act of self-determination fosters confidence and trust in yourself, which is essential to self-love. The more you learn to listen to your own needs, the more you recognize your own worth. You begin to see that you are deserving of the effort it takes to nurture your body and mind, and this realization strengthens the love you have for yourself.

Healing deepens when you begin to listen to your body instead of trying to manage it. Your body speaks to you in its own quiet way, through tension, fatigue, hunger, or restlessness. Every ache, every flutter of discomfort, every burst of energy is a form of communication. When you slow down long enough to pay attention, you start to recognize the patterns. You notice how your shoulders tighten when you feel pressured, how your stomach twists when something doesn't sit right, how your breathing changes when you're anxious or at peace. These are not random reactions. They are messages. Your body is always trying to tell you something about what it needs, what it fears, and what it longs for.

We are taught to silence these signals, to push through pain, to drink caffeine instead of resting, to smile instead of crying, to hold ourselves together instead of letting ourselves feel. Over time, that disconnection becomes a habit. You stop noticing what your body is saying until it finally shouts through exhaustion, burnout, or illness. Listening to your body means breaking that cycle. It means paying attention before the warning signs become unbearable. It means noticing the small whispers before they turn into demands. The more you listen, the more fluent you become in its language.

Start by asking questions instead of making assumptions. What is this tension trying to tell me? What am I holding here that I haven't let go of? What would feel comforting right now? Sometimes the body needs movement. Sometimes it needs stillness. Sometimes it needs food or water. Sometimes it simply needs permission to rest or to be acknowledged. The answers won't always come in words. They might come as a sigh of relief, a deep breath, or a sense of release in your muscles. Over time, you begin to trust those cues. You start to realize that your body is not working against you; it is guiding you toward balance.

This kind of awareness transforms how you care for yourself. Instead of moving through life on autopilot, you begin to live in partnership with your body. You choose foods, activities, and habits that support it rather than punish it. You rest because you feel the difference it makes, not because you've earned it. You move because your body wants to be expressed, not because you're trying to change it. When you learn to listen, healing becomes less about control and more about connection. You begin to understand that your body has always known the way forward. It has been speaking to you all along, waiting for the moment you would finally listen.

Over time, this practice becomes an act of devotion. You begin to sense when your body needs movement and when it needs stillness. You notice how it responds to nourishment, how it relaxes when you give it care, and how it thanks you in ways that words never could. Reparenting your body is not about perfection; it is about partnership. It is the process of remembering that your body is not your enemy—it is your oldest friend. It has been with you through every chapter, waiting for you to come home to it again.

When you start to treat your body with that kind of compassion, everything changes. You stop chasing perfection and start nurturing peace. You begin to feel safe within your own skin again. This safety becomes the foundation for growth, healing, and confidence. It allows your heart, mind, and body to move in the same direction, supporting each other instead of working against one another. This journey is also about creating alignment between your mental and physical states. When you nurture both your body and mind, you allow them to work together in harmony.

This unity is key to building self-love because it removes the disconnect between how you feel physically and emotionally. When you make choices that support your health, you're not just improving your physical appearance; you're enhancing your mental clarity and emotional well-being. The love you give yourself through these actions nurtures both your body and your mind, creating a powerful cycle of growth and healing.

The most powerful form of love is trust. When you learn to trust yourself, you stop living on guard. You stop questioning every decision, second-guessing your instincts, or waiting for someone else to tell you what to do. Trust is the quiet confidence that you will be there for yourself, no matter how uncertain life becomes. It grows through patience and repetition. You build it each time you keep your promises to yourself, each time you show up for yourself, even when it's easier to turn away. It does not come from perfection or control. It comes from reliability, from the promise that you will not abandon yourself when things get hard.

Self-trust is the connection that ties your mind, body, and heart together. Your mind creates the intention, your heart gives it meaning, and your body turns it into movement. When all three are in harmony, you feel grounded and whole. When one part falters, the others rise to help you steady yourself. You build this harmony in small, quiet ways. It happens when you choose rest over exhaustion, when you speak kindly instead of criticizing yourself, and when you act on what feels right to you, even if no one else understands. Each of those moments strengthens the thread between your inner parts, weaving them into something solid and unbreakable.

This kind of love is not about being perfect. It is about being faithful. It means trusting that you can forgive yourself when you make mistakes and believing you can recover when you fall short. Every time you keep a promise to yourself, you send a message to your body that it can rely on you. You tell your heart that its feelings matter and your mind that it can rest without needing to control everything. That is what true alignment feels like. It is a steady rhythm between thought, feeling, and action that creates peace from within. Love becomes something you practice instead of chase, a way of living that strengthens over time.

Ultimately, self-love is about building a lasting relationship with yourself. It is about learning to stand by your own side with the same loyalty you offer to the people you love most. When you trust yourself, you no longer need constant reassurance or approval. You move through life with quiet confidence, knowing that no matter what happens, you will handle it with grace. That is what it means to live in partnership with yourself—to love, trust, and believe in the person you already are.

Just as you would care for a loved one, it's important to care for yourself with kindness, patience, and understanding. This means accepting where you are in your journey, acknowledging your needs, and giving yourself the grace to grow. As you continue to align your health with your mental clarity and physical well-being, you will find that the love you give yourself will reflect to you in profound ways. Self-love is the foundation for all the healing and growth you seek, and it's the most powerful tool you have to create a life of balance, peace, and happiness.

Forgive yourself for both your past and your present. Stand in front of the mirror and show kindness to the person you see reflected. It's easy to get caught up in self-criticism, but remember, the way you treat yourself matters most. We are living in a time when body positivity is celebrated like never before. The narrative around beauty is shifting, and now, more than ever, we see diverse bodies being embraced and appreciated in all their forms. No longer do you have to hide or feel ashamed of your body because it doesn't fit some outdated standard.

Today, we see bodies of all shapes and sizes being highlighted in ways they've never been before. Whether it's the scars that tell your story, the rolls that signify a life well-lived, or the cellulite that shows the truth of your body's natural texture, these once-taboo features are now front and center on billboards, in commercials, and even on fashion runways. The media and culture are beginning to reflect the reality that beauty is not one-size-fits-all. This evolution is an invitation for you to embrace your body without shame or guilt, acknowledging that you are worthy of love exactly as you are, no matter what.

Confidence begins when you stop asking for permission to be yourself. Real confidence comes from knowing you belong here, just as you are. It's the calm that settles in when you stop apologizing for the space you take up. It's not about appearance or perfection. It's about presence. When you start carrying yourself with self-respect, something shifts. You move with intention. You speak without shrinking. You show up knowing that your worth doesn't depend on anyone else seeing it first.

Confidence isn't loud. It doesn't need to be announced or performed. It grows quietly every time you listen to your intuition and follow through on what feels right for you. It builds each time you stop comparing yourself to others and focus on your own rhythm. It strengthens when you let yourself rest without guilt or express your needs without fear. The more you live in alignment with who you are, the more natural confidence feels.

True confidence is what happens when your body, mind, and heart begin working in concert instead of against each other. Your thoughts stop tearing you down, your body relaxes, and your heart opens. You start to feel steady inside your own skin. You trust your choices. You stop trying to prove your worth and begin living from it. Confidence isn't built by fixing yourself. It comes from finally accepting that there was never anything broken to begin with.

You'll know you've reached this kind of confidence when it starts to feel effortless. You walk differently. You laugh without holding back. You say what you mean without fear of how it will sound. You extend kindness to others without losing yourself in the process. This is confidence that doesn't need approval because it comes from truth.

When you start to look at yourself through the lens of gratitude, something inside you loosens. The pressure to measure up to old versions of yourself fades away. You stop comparing your current reflection to memories of the past and start seeing the value in who you have become. You begin to recognize how much your body has carried you through, how many times your heart has healed after being broken, and how your mind has learned to see the world with more understanding. Gratitude transforms regret into perspective. It softens harsh self-criticism and reminds you that every season of your life has played a part in shaping the person you are now. Even the moments that once felt unbearable have added depth to your compassion and resilience.

Growth is not something to conceal or minimize. It deserves to be acknowledged. You have changed because you were meant to, and those changes are the marks of your becoming. You have grown stronger because you faced what once scared you. You have become gentler because you learned to forgive. You have developed patience because life taught you to wait for what is real.

Healing takes time, and it asks for patience. It is not a straight path with clear signs or easy directions. There will be days when it feels as though you are moving backward, when the progress you have made seems to vanish, and when the weight of it all feels heavy again. In those moments, remember that this is part of the process. Healing moves in waves. It expands and contracts like the tide, sometimes strong and steady, sometimes still and unseen.

Your journey toward self-love belongs only to you. It will not look like anyone else's, and it should not have to. No one else can feel what you feel or understand your body the way you do. This is your path, and it will unfold in its own rhythm. Trust your inner voice when it tells you to slow down, to rest, or to begin again. Listen when your body asks for care and your heart asks for peace. They will guide you in the right direction if you allow them to. You do not have to rush or prove anything to anyone. The power you are looking for is already within you. It grows stronger every time you choose to treat yourself with honesty, respect, and compassion. When you love and listen to yourself, you move closer to the balance and strength you have always been capable of.

As you continue on this journey, remind yourself that it is not about reaching some final version of who you think you should be. It is about embracing the person you already are in this moment. There is no perfect time to begin loving yourself, no milestone you must reach first, no number on a scale or achievement that will finally make you ready. The only moment that exists is this one. Right here, right now, you have the power to turn toward yourself with love.

Whether you are just beginning to explore what self-love even means or you have been walking this path for years, know that every effort counts. The love you are learning to give yourself will ripple through everything you do. It will soften the way you speak to yourself, change how you handle challenges, set an example for those around you, and even shift the energy you bring into your relationships.

Let yourself release what you have been carrying. The shame that tells you you're behind, the guilt that whispers you should be more, the old judgments that keep you small—you do not need any of it anymore. You have done enough, tried enough, and been enough. This is the moment to step into your potential, not as someone chasing a standard set by others but as someone finally deciding to honor who they already are.

You are allowed to take up space in your own life. You are allowed to be proud of how far you have come, even if the world has not noticed. You are worthy of love right now, not once you have changed, not when you have achieved more, but exactly as you are. When you begin to believe that, your entire life starts to shift. The weight of striving begins to lift, and what takes its place is peace—the kind that grows from self-acceptance.

The journey of self-love is not about becoming perfect. It is about learning to stay with yourself through the imperfect parts. It is about progress, about small steps that no one else sees but that matter deeply. Each morning you choose kindness over criticism, each night you let yourself rest without guilt, you are building a relationship with yourself that is based on care rather than control. This is how healing happens. It happens through the steady commitment to treat yourself like someone worth loving. You are. You always have been. Your body has been loyal through every season of your life. It has kept your heart beating, your lungs moving, your feet carrying you forward. It has asked for nothing but care in return. Now is the time to give it that care. You do not need to reshape yourself to be worthy of love. You do not need to fit into someone else's definition of beauty. You are already complete. You are already enough.

Move through this process one moment at a time, with patience and compassion. Healing and growth are not sudden awakenings. They unfold slowly, through choices that honor your well-being. Every act of self-love—every meal eaten with intention, every breath taken to calm your thoughts, every time you choose rest over punishment—moves you closer to balance. As you learn to nurture yourself fully, your body begins to relax, your mind becomes clearer, and your spirit feels stronger. You start to see that love is not something you find outside of yourself. It has been within you all along, waiting to be remembered. When you embrace every part of who you are—the soft, the strong, the uncertain, and the brave—you discover that you already have everything you need to live fully. Nothing can stop a person who finally decides to love themselves completely.

Chapter 12

Turning toward Family

Seeking Comfort without Fear

Family—whether it's the one you were born with or the one you've chosen, can sometimes be the greatest and most daunting thing to consider when it comes to opening up about a traumatic experience. The people closest to us are often the ones we fear disappointing or burdening, which makes it difficult to voice our pains. There's this unspoken pressure to maintain harmony with them because they aren't going anywhere, and you can't really hide from them without cutting yourself off completely. Naturally, we want to protect them from uncomfortable truths to avoid being met with skepticism or judgment, or to avoid the topic being the next dinner conversation that happens repeatedly for three weeks.

Cultural and familial expectations can add another layer of complexity, too. These expectations might look like demands for you to have better emotional resilience or for you to not talk about it or have a reaction to anything. The idea that "family sticks together no matter what" becomes a challenge. Some families prioritize maintaining appearances or suppressing difficult emotions, creating an environment where sharing pain feels like a betrayal.

It's safe to assume that we all know that some cultures might follow more traditional values, while others lean more toward modern beliefs. I'm not saying either one is right or wrong, but it's something to consider when you're preparing to open up about trauma. A traditional family might expect you not to get anyone involved or for your conversation not to leave the four walls of the room, while a family with more modern beliefs might urge you to seek help or turn outward for support. On top of that, it's important to make a note of the age gap as well.

Generational differences often shape how families respond to trauma. In many households, silence means strength, and anything that disrupts the family image is quickly muffled and pushed aside. The fact of the matter is that many of our older generations were taught to keep matters private and that most things that are more than casual conversation are for behind closed doors only, and *most definitely* not to be spoken about at the dinner table. Disclosure of emotions or hard experiences feels like a violation of an unspoken rule. Unfortunately, that belief gets passed down with the intent of being helpful rather than harmful.

The gap becomes clear when younger family members try to bring up trauma and are met with confusion or dismissal. Instead of open ears, they get a "Shhh, it's not that big a deal" or "I'm sure they didn't mean it like that." What starts out as an act of courage to you might feel unnecessary and disruptive to someone raised with different values. Even worse, they could urge you to keep quiet out of protection for those involved, trying to downplay the fact that you're a victim or survivor and instead trying to protect all parties.

On the contrary, it's possible that your family may have had a more difficult upbringing than you or they may be more tolerant of certain behaviors. You discussing things that have been traumatic to you may seem silly to them. They may believe you're being spoiled or high maintenance and insinuate that you don't know what "real problems" look like.

It doesn't mean your pain is any less real, but it does explain why the response might not match what you'd hoped for. Understanding that their reaction is shaped by their upbringing, and not their lack of care for you, can take some of the sting out of it.

Here's another example. In some cultures, there's an emphasis on respecting elders without question or prioritizing unity over individuality. Therefore, if an elder was involved in your trauma, others might fear you'll be told you were wrong because you are not listening to and respecting your elders. Even worse, you're disrespecting them by talking about them this way. These values make vulnerability feel dangerous, as if speaking honestly about your experience risks dishonoring the family itself. While these norms might have once been tools for survival in hard times, they can leave little room for any kind of messy truth.

Generational divides also influence how people see mental health. Younger generations often talk openly about therapy, boundaries, and healing, while older relatives might see those concepts as unnecessary, weak, or even indulgent. After all, they grew up with their own trauma and turned out *perfectly fine*, so why should you need them?

Don't you hate it when people say that?

These contrasts create friction and misunderstanding toward topics that they were never taught to understand or consider. It's not necessarily their fault; they just weren't raised in a world where there was so much emphasis on mental health. Nowadays, you can take a "mental health day" off work without getting blinked at—but fifty years ago, you'd get questioned and fired. A good work ethic meant showing up and doing the job day in and day out without letting anything derail your course. Bridging these differences is possible, but it just isn't the easiest. You can't force people to see things your way. Getting through these hurdles will mean you have to recognize the lens they're viewing life through while still being strong and respecting your own need to be heard.

You might not be able to change their perspective at all, but you can chip away a little bit of space for your truth. Have an understanding of their values and talk to them about that. Bring it up in the conversation that you understand they might not see things your way or understand why this is an issue but that it is important to you, and that's what matters.

A huge part of healing is about breaking cycles—especially when it means being the first in your family to speak out about something. That being said, breaking cycles is, well, exactly as it sounds. It's a cycle. When something has been done a certain way for generations, it's not easy to be the first person to step out of that norm and choose a different route. It can make people feel angry, embarrassed, resentful, or even make them feel like you are suggesting that you are better than them.

On the contrary, let's say you choose not to break the cycle and keep things to yourself. Well, leaving trauma to be unspoken can be just as isolating as the trauma itself. There's no need for you to take on the weight and convince yourself you don't need anyone's help. You don't need to be a superhero; it's unnecessary. Admitting what happened takes a lot of courage—especially when you have no idea how the ones you love will react. Will they believe you? Will they dismiss or downplay your pain? Will they think you're overreacting? Will they tell you it's all really not a big deal?

These uncertainties create an imaginary barrier that makes it feel safer to stay silent and carry the burden alone. The fear of rejection and misjudgment makes the isolation feel worse and makes the conversation feel like a huge moment. Unfortunately, you have to break the silence for your own safety. Keeping it to yourself can create spiraling, and that comes with great dangers for you. As I said before, it's completely unnecessary.

Being seen differently after sharing a traumatic experience can be overwhelming and scary. We have egos and self-respect to uphold, and admitting you lost control of a situation can make you feel small. You might also feel guilt and dread, as if speaking up can lead to punishment or reprimand. It's normal to battle with this. This feeling can be especially intense during adolescence because your vulnerability is already heightened by your search for identity and a sense of belonging. The fear that revealing your trauma might change how your family sees you or create a divide that feels insurmountable can make silence feel like the only option.

You might also fear an overreaction: immediate involvement from the people involved, the authorities, extended family, or even school officials adds weight to the conversation. It makes you feel you might lose control over a situation again.

Once you've moved forward or finally found the strength to open up, you then have to worry about how the process of opening up might become traumatic on its own. Loved ones might react with shock, stress, anger, or urgency that feels overwhelming. While these reactions are usually well-intended and are signs someone cares about you, you might take them harshly. For a person already emotionally unprepared to process everything, this creates more obstacles instead of support.

Navigating the weight of your own emotions while also managing others' responses is a delicate balance. Facing these past struggles is hard enough on its own, and doing so in an environment where emotions run high can make it really hard. This is why timing and emotional safety are crucial when opening up and navigating these conversations. Ideally—a safe space should be created, one where both parties can manage their emotional responses without feeling overwhelmed. In simpler terms, it's not about only what you say but the environment where you say it.

When you disclose trauma to your family, they aren't just hearing about your experience. They now also have to confront what all of this means for them. While this obviously isn't as traumatic for them as it is for you, it's still hard to hear and can be painful. This can stir up something called secondary trauma, which is when the loved one you're speaking with feels triggered, shocked, guilty, or even has a sense of grief just from exposure to your story. The intensity of your truth forces them to face unexpected emotions they couldn't prepare for. If they are caught off guard, their reaction can spill out in a way they don't intend. Sometimes, they need time to process what you've told them before they can support you, and that should not be considered selfish. It's just part of the process.

Defensiveness is also a common response. A parent might feel crushed by guilt for not noticing what was happening. They might feel like a failure that they were unable to protect you. Instead of owning that pain, they might deny or minimize yours. They might feel angry, like they "raised you better," depending on the specifics of the scenario.

A sibling might feel helpless, so their response might be to lash out, brush past things quickly, or shut down. Maybe the same trauma happened to them, and they didn't handle it the way you are, so they dismiss your experience.

Reactions like this are not an indicator of whether your trauma is valid. They are signs your disclosure is bringing up your family's own unresolved emotions. Imagine if someone came up to you in confidence, asked to speak, and then told you a story incredibly similar to your experience. It would probably be difficult to set your emotions aside and listen fully. That might be what your family is going through.

These defensive reactions ultimately feel like rejection. You've taken a big risk and worked up the courage to share, and hearing "That can't be true" or suggestions that you're exaggerating can cut deep. It's important to recognize that these responses come from fear or shame, not lack of love. It doesn't make them okay by any means, but it helps you understand that resistance is about their discomfort.

Secondary trauma can also lead to overreaction. Instead of denial, certain family members throw themselves into crisis mode, trying to fix everything immediately. This is one reason many victims don't share—they fear the involvement of the authorities or the possibility of a family member taking revenge. Your loved one might threaten to harm someone or contact them directly instead of stopping to give you the care you need at that moment. Maybe they want to pick up the phone or shoot off an angry text. Their sense of urgency is them wanting to undo your harm, but it leaves you carrying the weight of your emotions *and* theirs at the same time.

Some relatives need time to process before they can meet you with empathy and kindness. Others might never move past defensiveness. Either way, own your truth. Do not warp it to tame their responses. Understanding this dynamic allows you to protect yourself emotionally while still allowing space for the people capable of growing into better supporters.

It's important to pause and remember that your family members are human too. They'll experience a full range of emotions, just like you. Just as it takes time and courage to speak about trauma, it takes time and courage to absorb it. Their initial reaction does not mean they won't eventually support and understand.

The key is to give yourself and your family time to process, knowing progress will be gradual. Everyone will ultimately move from shock to acceptance.

Disclosure rarely happens in one moment, unless you blurt it out at the dinner table. Most of the time, it unfolds in stages. You might start with vague hints—like saying you aren't in a good mood or maybe your family simply notices you've been acting differently. This first area of opening up is like testing the waters. This is when you test what feels safe and who might be safest to open up to. It's where you see how your family starts to react to vulnerability.

If the initial response feels good and supportive, the next stage typically involves sharing a piece of your story but not the whole thing. It's like the "We broke up" without the "They cheated on me and stole my money and made me feel unsafe" side of the story. It's not the entire event but just enough to gauge their potential reaction and whether they can handle the whole story. This stage helps you build confidence and create a foundation of trust and understanding. There's no time limit on this part; just pay attention to your emotions, and if you decide you need more time, absolutely take it.

The final stage is full honesty, but should be done only when and if you feel ready. At this stage, the environment and your own readiness matter just as much as the words. By approaching your full disclosure in small layers, you maintain control over your story and protect yourself from being overwhelmed. It allows you to pace the process in a way that honors your own needs.

Think about how you would like to guide the conversation. Consider setting boundaries and voicing what you need from your listeners—whether it's an open ear, patience, help, or action. Being clear about your needs from the start helps lay the foundation for more compassionate and patient responses.

You can also set the tone for the conversation by doing it somewhere quiet and private. Bringing listeners out of their normal habitat into a more serious setting gives them the mental signal to really tune in and listen, whereas sitting in the living room with the TV on and dogs barking or nieces and nephews running around might catch them off guard when the conversation turns serious. Bringing them somewhere secluded indicates they need to give you their undivided attention.

It can be helpful to educate or offer context for what you're going through, especially if your trauma is not easily understood or recognized by others. Letting others know how to best support you can create a space for a more understanding and nonjudgmental response. If they do not have the tools to fully process or react in a helpful way, guiding them with patience can foster a more positive interaction.

Telling them your hopes for the conversation also prevents you from being let down unexpectedly. You can make up scenarios in your head about how the conversation should go, but if it doesn't happen that way—it can be discouraging. This is not fair to you or them and sets everyone up for failure.

Once you've shared what you're going through, boundaries become even more important. These conversations might open the door to lots of questions, opinions, unsolicited advice, and pressure you don't want or need. Some family members might want every detail right away, while others might bring it up repeatedly when you're not ready for it. Setting limits—like saying "I don't want to discuss this anymore right now" isn't you being rude; it's you protecting your peace. You don't owe anyone 100 percent of your time, stories, or emotions.

Boundaries need to include how you want your story handled outside the conversation. You have the right to ask relatives not to repeat what you've shared or discuss it with anyone, including family and friends. If someone ignores those boundaries, it tells you about their character, and I'd urge you to step back from that person.

The idea of setting a boundary is not to push family away and keep secrets but rather to create a safety net for yourself. Boundaries give a clear structure to the relationship, allowing you to stay connected with the person without feeling exposed and anxious. Trauma already strips away a sense of control; boundaries are your way of reclaiming it and making sure that feeling doesn't get worse.

More often than not, family members will be the first to sense when something is off with you and that something might have happened. They typically have the best radars on your mood and energy. You might be surprised to find they are already waiting for you to ask to have a conversation because they suspected a problem. They might have even had conversations with one another, asking if anyone knows what's troubling you.

The phrase "elephant in the room" exists for a reason; when unspoken tension lingers, it's felt by everyone. Though you've probably done your best to remain calm and hide what's going on, I guarantee your family has felt the energy shift. Even if your family hasn't confronted you directly, they might have hinted at their concerns or even repeatedly asked if everything is okay, unsure of how to navigate this shift.

It can feel annoying at this stage. If your family won't leave you alone and keeps asking what's wrong, try to be patient and give them some grace. It's a blessing to have people close enough to you to notice you're not doing well. When preparing to open up, recognizing that they could already be waiting might help lighten some pressure.

Now, what if the trauma comes from the family itself? Honesty is such a huge step in moving forward, but what if the family in question is literally the reason you're in this predicament in the first place? When the trauma comes from within the family itself, disclosure takes on a new level of complexity. Speaking up now feels like you're turning against the people you're expected to trust and protect. The fear of being labeled disloyal or ungrateful makes silence feel like the better option. Naming harm done by a relative can be treated as betrayal when it's simply the truth.

You might find yourself torn between needing support and knowing your family is not a safe place to find it. Some relatives might outright deny your experience, while others excuse it or minimize it to avoid conflict. They expect you to understand "That's just the way someone is"; therefore, your feelings aren't valid. Questioning and discouragement can make you question your own memories and instincts and create a cycle of doubt.

Try to separate the individual relationships from the larger family tree. Just because the trauma involved a particular family member doesn't mean the entire family is unsafe and toxic. Some relatives might still be capable of offering care and concern, while others remain tied to that dysfunction.

It's easy assume some family members might be guilty by association. Think about whether or not, in these situations, the person truly *is* guilty, knows everything that happened, and is okay with it. Take time to pay attention to each family member and try to distinguish who can be trusted and who you need to protect yourself from. This allows you to still have conversations within the family, though your circle might be smaller than you'd like.

Unfortunately, sometimes distance is safest. Walking away from harmful relatives is not weak or petty; it's survival. You do not have to maintain contact with people who continue to harm you simply because you share blood or a last name. Protecting your safety and well-being is far more important than preserving a relationship out of expectation. If choosing to step back will have more benefits and healing effects for you personally, you have to be selfish and do it. Many times, creating distance can be the beginning of a healthier family relationship, as it forces people to understand and consider things they've done.

Healing turns into you defining family on your own terms. That might mean confiding in or finding strength from your chosen family, friends, or community who respect your truth. It means building boundaries that keep you safe and protected while you sort through the damage. The point is not to force reconciliation where it isn't possible and to free yourself from the idea that healing requires reunion.

If this isn't the case for you, then family can play a crucial role in your healing. They can offer support, understanding, and a sense of belonging. Whether it's the family you're born into or the family you've chosen, having people who care about your well-being can provide the foundation needed to process pain and move forward.

All these emotional wounds can be isolating, but knowing you have a support system—people who genuinely want to see you heal—can make the process less overwhelming. Even when family members don't fully understand what you've been through, their presence and willingness to listen can make a difference. Some family members might offer support through verbal comfort, while others might express support through actions like cooking a meal, cleaning your house, even running your errands. These are small actions that show you that you aren't alone.

If you find yourself to be someone who needs to lean on chosen family, that support can be special. The strength of chosen family lies in freedom. These relationships exist because of mutual care, not obligation. Honesty feels easier and support comes without strings. When someone chooses to stand by you, their presence affirms your worth in a deeply healing way. Chosen family can help ease disappointment if your biological family isn't able to be the support you need.

Equally important, chosen family can balance what's missing at home. They can be the ones you call after a hard disclosure or the ones who remind you of your progress and sit with you in silence when words feel too heavy. When you broaden your definition of *family* to include more than just blood relatives, you give yourself permission to form strong bonds with people and find truly safe connection. Family is not always about who *should* be there but about who actually shows up.

One of the most valuable aspects of being able to lean on your family is the stability they can offer during times of emotional distress. Through all your doubts, setbacks, and frustrations, a strong family presence can serve as a reminder that you are simply not alone. Whether it's a reassuring conversation, a shared meal in silence, or just having their company under the same roof, there's a natural comfort. Family can offer you grounding when it feels like the world around you is falling apart.

Family can also help with accountability and push you to continue taking steps toward recovery when you're feeling over it. They can give you tough love. They can remind you of your progress, help you seek professional support if that's what is needed, and motivate you to engage in self-care. Healing requires facing painful truths and having people who gently (or aggressively) continue to push you toward growth rather than allowing you to stay stuck in your pain is invaluable. Family is your mirror, reflecting your struggles and your resilience, and helping you see the strength within. Accountability can feel harsh, but it's nurturing. Progress is progress.

Opening up about trauma can leave you emotionally drained, even if the conversation goes exactly how you want. The buildup of fear, the act of speaking and revisiting things, and the uncertainty of how everyone will respond can take a toll. Prepare by planning a self-care routine, something that can help soften the crash that often follows tough conversations.

Self-care after sharing doesn't need to be elaborate; it can be simple. Sometimes it's as simple as giving yourself quiet time, going for a walk, taking a bubble bath, or journaling what you're feeling. These small actions can help release the intensity that lingers once the adrenaline wears off and can help you feel better about being exposed. Choose something that can ground you, make you feel steady again, and allow you to release some emotions privately.

This helps set up support outside that hard conversation. Knowing you have an additional layer of support waiting keeps you from feeling stranded if the family response isn't what you needed. Not to mention, it can give your family time to process as well, without them feeling they need to sit there with you for an undesignated amount of time because they don't know how else to react or what to say.

Before sharing, deciding what you'll do afterward shifts your mindset and reminds you there is more to life after the conversation. It's a gentle reminder that the conversation won't last forever, and when you're ready for it to be over, you can say something like, "Well, I'm going to take a bubble bath for a few minutes," to signal you need a moment.

The bottom line is that caring for yourself after opening up is part of the process. Tending to yourself before and afterward creates a rhythm of protection and keeps you moving forward.

At its core—the role of family in healing is connection, knowing you are seen, valued, and supported as you work through your pain. Clear and open communication is key to helping your family support you. Be vocal about what would help you most during this time, whether that's receiving emotional support, space to process things on your own, or even acknowledgment of what happened and no further mention of it.

Your family is more than just a part of your life—they are quite literally connected to you, sharing not only history but an unspoken bond that often runs deeper than words. No matter the circumstances, most families genuinely want to help in any way they can, even if they have no idea how. Allow them to be there for you, to offer guidance, and to provide the support you need as you navigate your healing journey. Lean on them as often as you can, embrace their love, and recognize that while they might not have all the answers, their presence can be a source of comfort and strength.

Chapter 13

Friendship's Healing Touch

Leaning on the Right People

Ah, the unofficial therapists of our lives—our true friends.

These are the people who listen without judgment, offering a safe space to unload both life's heaviest burdens and the smallest everyday frustrations. They are the ones you turn to first, the ones who hear your unfiltered thoughts and feelings before anyone else. When trauma shakes your world, they are often the first to know, providing comfort in ways that feel natural and unforced.

Sometimes their presence alone feels like a kind of healing. Just knowing they're there can remind you that you don't have to carry everything by yourself, even when life feels unbearably heavy. Their words, spoken gently and without pressure, can pull you back from places you thought you'd never escape. They remind you that healing is still possible, even when the path forward feels endless. Maybe the most beautiful thing of all is how they manage to make you laugh again, often before you even realize you're ready. In those moments, you catch a glimpse of yourself returning, piece by piece, reminding you that light can still exist in the middle of pain.

Friendships are a vital part of the healing process, often providing a kind of support that can't be found anywhere else. While family might offer unconditional love, friends have a unique ability to meet you where you are without the complexities that sometimes come with familial relationships. They are the ones who know you in your truest form, accepting your flaws, celebrating your strengths, and standing by you during the darkest of times. Their understanding, rooted in shared experiences and mutual respect, allows them to offer insights and perspectives that can be profoundly healing.

Sometimes their role is simply to give you room to be yourself, without expectations or pressure. When you're weighed down by trauma or just need someone to listen, real friends offer a place that feels safe and steady. In their company, honesty comes easily because you know you won't be judged or dismissed. They become your shelter in the storm, the place where you can exhale and let the noise of the world fade for a while. In their presence, you feel seen and accepted exactly as you are, and that kind of understanding brings a sense of peace that words rarely can.

After trauma, isolation often starts to feel like the safest place to hide. Pulling away can seem easier than risking another wound or another moment of being misunderstood. In the beginning, solitude feels like control. It gives you space to breathe, to collect yourself, to exist without anyone watching or asking questions. For a while, that space feels necessary. But over time, the stillness begins to change. What once brought comfort starts to press against you, and the quiet that once soothed you begins to ache. You start to notice how much distance you've built between yourself and the world. Laughter sounds different, connection feels far away, and you realize how easy it is to get lost in your own silence.

This is where friendship begins to find its way back in. Sometimes it starts with a simple text that says, *Thinking of you,* or a quick visit that breaks through the stillness of your day. Those small moments can spark something inside you, reminding you that love hasn't disappeared from your world. Reconnection doesn't come with fanfare; it slips in gently, the way sunlight finds its way through a half-closed curtain. It's the quiet courage to answer a message, say yes to coffee, or let someone sit beside you when you'd rather be alone. Every time you choose to reach back, even in the smallest way, you remind yourself that safety can exist beyond the walls you built to survive.

Sometimes, a friend's role in your healing journey is to be a mirror, reflecting your pain but also your strength. They might see the resilience within you when you can't, reminding you how far you've come, even when it feels like you've taken a step back. It is often difficult to see beyond the shadows of trauma, especially when you're in the midst of it. Friends are the ones who can gently lift you above your pain, showing you the bigger picture and reminding you of your inherent strength. During moments of doubt, when the weight of your experiences threatens to overwhelm you, friends can offer words of encouragement that give you the strength to keep moving forward.

Their genuine belief in you can be a powerful motivator, especially when your own confidence is shaken. A simple text or phone call can be enough to pull you back from the edge, reminding you that you are worthy of support and healing. Their confidence in your potential often acts like a beacon, shining light on your path even when the darkness seems all-consuming. Sometimes, friends can also offer wisdom or a fresh perspective that shifts your entire outlook on the situation, turning what seemed like an insurmountable challenge into a manageable hurdle.

Friendship often mirrors the way you see yourself. The kind of people you draw in, and the way they treat you, reflect how you view your own worth. If you've learned to tolerate being mistreated, you might find yourself surrounded by people who keep that pattern alive. If you've always been the one who listens, fixes, or smooths things over, it can be hard to notice when your own needs are being overlooked. Healing asks you to look more closely at these patterns and to start asking honest questions. Do the people around you make you feel calm and valued, or do they leave you drained and second-guessing yourself? Do they give as much as they take? The answers to those questions often reveal what you truly believe you deserve, and changing that belief is one of the most powerful steps in your healing.

As you begin to value yourself more, your friendships start to change. You stop settling for connections that are rooted in convenience or obligation, and you begin to crave something more authentic. The friends who truly belong in your life will celebrate this growth instead of being threatened by it. They'll meet you in your higher standard of love, offering the same respect and honesty you've learned to offer yourself. This is where the mirror becomes a tool for transformation rather than reflection.

Every healthy friendship is proof that you are worthy of kindness without needing to earn it. It reminds you that real connection doesn't come from trying to be perfect or giving more than you have. It grows from honesty, mutual care, and the willingness to show up as you are. The friends who reflect your worth back to you are gentle reminders of how far you've come, of how much you've grown, and of the self-respect that now shapes the way you let people love you. They show you what it looks like to be valued simply for being yourself, and that realization changes everything.

At times, friends know exactly what you need without you having to say a word. They have a way of sensing when you're struggling, even if you've tried to hide it. Whether it's offering a comforting word, a shoulder to cry on, or simply showing up with your favorite comfort food, friends seem to have an uncanny ability to provide exactly what you need at particular moments. Their intuition and empathy can fill the gaps in your healing process, helping you navigate the most difficult parts of your journey.

There's something incredibly healing about having someone who just "gets it"—who can walk into your world without needing an explanation, yet who knows exactly how to help. When words fall short, their actions can speak volumes. Sometimes, just knowing someone truly understands what you're going through can be the catalyst for beginning to heal. It can feel like a weight lifts, not because the trauma has gone away but because someone sees you, and that recognition can make all the difference.

Some friendships are defined by words, while others are defined by presence. The friend who stays through silence offers a kind of healing that can't be put into language. They sit beside you during hard days, unbothered by the quiet, unafraid of your stillness. They don't fill the space with advice or platitudes; they simply exist with you in it. That shared silence becomes a language of its own—a way of saying, "I see you," without you needing to explain what hurts.

There's something sacred about that kind of companionship. In their stillness, you feel permission to stop performing strength; you release the need to appear okay. You learn that love doesn't always look like fixing—it often looks like sitting. The sound of their steady breathing, the warmth of their presence, the calm of knowing someone will stay no matter how long it takes—these are moments that begin to soften the edges of your pain.

After experiencing trauma, even the safest people can feel unsafe at first. You might find yourself second-guessing others' intentions or analyzing every small change in tone or expression. This hyperawareness once protected you—it helped you survive an environment where safety wasn't guaranteed. The challenge now is that your body still responds as if danger is everywhere, even when it's not. Learning to feel safe again isn't about forcing trust; it's about slowly teaching your body that not every connection leads to harm.

This relearning happens in small moments. It's when a friend shows consistency, follows through on their word, or listens without interrupting. It's when someone offers support without demanding anything in return. Over time, these small experiences begin to rewire what safety feels like. Your guard starts to lower naturally, not because someone convinced you to trust them but because they've shown you that trust is safe.

There will still be days when you pull back out of habit, when vulnerability feels like too much. That's okay. Healing doesn't mean erasing your protective instincts—it means learning when they're needed and when they're not. Every time you choose to stay open instead of shutting down, you teach yourself that love and connection can exist without fear.

When it feels like you can't pick yourself up, it's often a friend who does it for you. They might physically or emotionally pull you out of bed when the weight of your trauma feels too heavy. Whether it's offering to spend the day with you, gently nudging you to take the first small step toward healing, or simply sitting beside you until you feel ready to face the world again, friends have a unique way of offering both the push and the compassion needed to get you back on track.

They help you reframe your struggles, offering a fresh perspective that can turn what feels like a setback into an opportunity for growth. This support is not always about fixing things but about being with you through the process, walking beside you as you navigate each step. The most important thing a friend offers in those moments is not a solution but a willingness to just "be there" with you, no matter how long it takes for healing to take root.

Ultimately, friendships are not just about sharing joy and laughter—they are also about standing together through the storms. A true friend is there for you when the path feels uncertain, providing stability when everything else feels unstable. They help you process emotions, guide you through the difficult days, and offer a reminder that you are not alone. Even when everything feels like it's unraveling, their steadfast support serves as a constant reminder that you're not walking this journey alone.

Before you lean on your friends for support during your healing process, it's essential to make sure you have the right people in your circle. Friendship should be a relationship built on trust, understanding, and mutual respect—not one bound by conditions or expectations. You should never feel pressured to act in a certain way, believe in something, or do things you're not comfortable with just to keep a friend. A true friend will never use your trauma against you, blame you for what you've been through, or make you feel small or invalid. They will lift you up, not drag you down. It's also important to remember that your friendships should not be based on obligation. A friend who truly values you will never make you feel as if you owe them something for their support.

Let me shout this from the rooftops: You are not obligated to keep someone in your life just because you've known them for years, they are family friends, or because they've been part of your past. Time does not automatically make someone a positive influence in your life. Just because you've known someone since childhood does not mean they are still the right fit for you decades later. The beauty of friendship, unlike family, is that you get to choose who stays in your life. In your healing journey, you simply cannot afford to invest energy in relationships that drain you or feel burdensome.

True friends will be the ones you are naturally drawn to, and you will feel their absence when they aren't around. Those are the people who will support and nourish you during your most important time of need. They will be the ones who gently guide you toward growth, challenging you when necessary but always with love and compassion.

People evolve as they grow, and sometimes those changes lead to shifts in relationships. It's important to recognize when a friendship no longer nurtures you or makes you feel good about yourself. If you reach the point where you feel it's time to step away from a friendship, it doesn't have to be dramatic or final. You don't have to burn any bridges, and it doesn't mean you can't reconnect down the line. Sometimes, the best thing for both people is to create some space, acknowledging that your paths or mindsets might no longer align as they once did. This is perfectly natural, and it doesn't reflect poorly on either person. What matters is that, at this moment in your life, you recognize the need for distance to protect your well-being. Relationships evolve, and sometimes we outgrow them, or they outgrow us. There's nothing wrong with that. In fact, it's often better to have a smaller, more tightly knit circle of people who truly support and understand you than to keep a large group of friends who might not be trustworthy or in tune with where you're at. Quality over quantity is key, especially when it comes to the relationships that will help you heal and grow.

Healing takes energy, and it's easy to forget that it also takes energy from the people who walk beside you. When you're hurting, it feels natural to lean on the friends who make you feel safe, the ones who understand without needing every detail. Still, it's important to notice when that leaning starts to turn into an imbalance. A healthy friendship has flow. It moves between giving and receiving, between listening and being heard. When one person is always the one holding space and the other is always the one being held, both start to feel tired. Real friendship feels like a rhythm, a quiet exchange where both hearts are seen and cared for. It's not about being perfectly even all the time. It's about having enough awareness to notice when things start to feel one-sided and gently finding your way back to balance.

This balance isn't about keeping score or measuring effort. It's about respect and awareness. A real friend doesn't count the times they've listened or shown up. They give because they care, not because they feel they have to. Still, part of honoring that love is remembering that they're human too. They have their own thoughts, feelings, and quiet struggles that deserve space and care. Recognizing that truth makes your connection softer, more honest, and more sustainable. When you show up for each other with that kind of awareness, the friendship becomes something that can last through anything.

Over time, this awareness strengthens the bond between you. It teaches you to be intentional about the energy you bring into the space you share. There will be moments when you're the one leaning and moments when you're the one holding. That exchange—the gentle give and take—is what keeps friendship alive through hard seasons. Healing isn't a one-sided act; it's a shared dance, and when both people honor that rhythm, love stays sustainable instead of exhausting.

Even the strongest, kindest friends can reach a point of emotional fatigue. This doesn't mean they care any less or that your pain is too much—it simply means they're human. Carrying someone else's emotions, especially over long periods, can be heavy, and sometimes people need to step back to recharge. This can feel personal when you're the one hurting, but it's not a reflection of your worth or their loyalty. It's a natural part of maintaining emotional health and respecting that space shows maturity and care on both sides.

Setting and respecting boundaries in friendship allow love to stay pure instead of becoming tangled in guilt or resentment. Healthy boundaries might look like shorter check-ins during emotionally intense seasons or openly saying, "I love you, but I need some space and time to myself for a little while." It might mean recognizing that sometimes your friend can't show up in the way you hoped, but that doesn't erase all the times they have. Boundaries are what allow relationships to breathe. They create a foundation where both people can support each other without burning out.

In many ways, boundaries are an act of love. They protect what's good within the friendship by ensuring neither person is stretched beyond their capacity. They also teach you to become more self-reliant over time, learning to comfort yourself rather than depending entirely on others to soothe your pain. When both people understand this rhythm, the friendship becomes stronger, built not on pressure but on genuine compassion that lasts.

A difficult reality for many people after experiencing trauma is the insensitivity they might encounter from certain friends. When someone hasn't gone through a life-altering or painful event, it can be easy for them to downplay or make light of your experience. This is something many people, including me, might have been guilty of before fully understanding the depth of trauma. In moments of comfort and familiarity, it's not uncommon for people to make jokes about sensitive or serious topics without realizing the impact their words have. Often, this comes from a lack of understanding, as they haven't experienced such pain themselves and can't grasp what it feels like.

Even for those who have been through something traumatic, humor can still serve as a coping mechanism. There are instances when people continue to make lighthearted jokes about sensitive subjects, not out of malice but as a way to process or find humor in their pain. They might try to see the silver lining or deflect the weight of their experiences with laughter. However, for those on the receiving end, this can feel hurtful, as the intention behind the jokes might not be clear. This highlights the importance of understanding the delicate balance between humor and respect, especially when navigating difficult or sensitive conversations with friends.

It's essential to approach these moments with empathy and awareness that not everyone processes pain the same way. What feels like comfort to one person might reopen a wound for another. Some people use humor to survive, to find small pieces of light in what once felt unbearable, while others need stillness and softness. True friends learn to read that difference. They listen with their hearts as much as their ears, paying attention to your tone, your silence, and the look in your eyes. They notice when laughter doesn't reach your eyes or when your body stiffens at a comment, and they adjust with care. It is a kind of emotional intuition, born out of love and patience. The people who truly see you will know when to sit in the quiet with you and when to lift the heaviness with gentle laughter. That sensitivity is what makes their presence feel like safety, and it is in those moments that the real depth of understanding in a friendship begins to show.

Even with the best intentions, the people we love most can sometimes stir our pain without realizing it. A single word, a familiar tone, or even a joke can pull you back into an old memory before you have time to brace yourself. One second, you're present and steady; the next, you're standing in the echo of something you thought you'd long outgrown. The confusion that follows can feel sharp and personal, leaving you wondering how someone who loves you could trigger something so raw.

Yet often, it isn't about the words themselves but about what those words awaken inside you. These moments become mirrors, reflecting the places where your healing still needs attention. They show you where tenderness is still required, where you still need gentleness instead of strength. Though uncomfortable, these moments are small windows into your own growth, invitations to understand yourself more fully, and reminders that healing is about awareness.

When this happens, it's easy to pull away and retreat into yourself. You might feel embarrassed for reacting or afraid that explaining will make things worse. Instead, try to pause and take a slow breath before responding. Ask yourself what's underneath the reaction. Is it fear, shame, sadness, or disappointment? Once you can name what you're feeling, you start to take your power back from it. That awareness lets you respond instead of just reacting.

When you bring that honesty into the friendship, it opens the door for real understanding. The right friend won't make you feel like you're too sensitive or that your pain is an inconvenience. They'll listen, take responsibility if necessary, and care enough to adjust because your comfort matters to them.

Moments like these can feel uncomfortable, but they often become turning points. They teach people how to stay connected even when things get hard. Every time you work through tension with empathy and honesty, your friendship grows stronger roots. A friend who can witness your reaction, hold space for it without judgment, and still choose to stay is showing you what real safety feels like. Those are the friendships that help you grow into someone who feels secure enough to love and be loved fully.

For many people, the shift in perspective after experiencing something traumatic can create distance between the victim of trauma and certain friends, especially if those friends continue to engage in behavior or discussions that feel insensitive. In this case, after a trauma, some victims found that certain friends continued to make political statements, share rants, or discuss topics that had become sincerely sensitive to them. It's important to remember that this wasn't necessarily the friend's fault.

The shift in perspective was personal—something that resulted from the experience—and it wasn't fair to expect friends to change their views or behaviors entirely to accommodate this new reality. What matters is recognizing that a change in perspective is a natural part of the healing process, and it's okay to honor that evolution within yourself. This understanding helps prevent resentment from building and allows you to navigate the changes in your friendships with compassion.

In moments like these, the most important thing is knowing when it's time to create distance. This doesn't mean you hold resentment or see someone as an enemy. It simply means you've recognized that a friendship no longer fits where you are right now. Sometimes taking care of yourself means stepping back, even from people you still care about. Choosing space isn't rejection; it's an act of protection. It's you honoring what you need to heal and giving yourself permission to move forward in peace. Letting go doesn't erase the good that once existed; it just means you're growing in a new direction. Healing doesn't require keeping every person from your past. Sometimes it asks you to release what no longer supports your peace so you can continue to grow in ways that feel right for you.

As you move through healing, it becomes more important to surround yourself with people who genuinely lift you up. Pay attention to how your body feels around them because your body often knows the truth before your mind does. Notice who makes you feel calm and safe and who leaves you uneasy or tense. You can feel it in the way your shoulders relax in comfort or tighten in discomfort. Those small reactions are signals that guide you toward what's good for you and away from what's not. When you start to listen to those cues, your circle might become smaller, but it will also become stronger. You'll find yourself surrounded by people who make you feel seen, grounded, and supported in all the right ways.

These physical responses can help you discern which friendships are nourishing and which ones might be draining. If being with someone leaves you feeling anxious, drained, or emotionally unsettled, it could be a sign that the relationship isn't serving you in the way you need. On the other hand, if you feel lighter, supported, and at peace in someone's presence, those are the friends to keep close.

Once you know who your people are—the ones who make you feel safe, seen, and genuinely cared for—lean into them completely. Let them know how much they mean to you. Show your gratitude instead of holding it back. These friends are the ones who remind you that love can still feel safe, even after pain. They'll bring laughter back into your days, help you find balance when everything feels heavy, and make life a little brighter just by being near. Their steadiness will become your anchor when things get hard, proof that you were never meant to go through any of this alone.

With the right people by your side, your path to healing will feel much more navigable, making every challenge a bit easier to overcome. As you continue to heal, your friendships will evolve with you, growing stronger and deeper as you do. The bonds you share with these friends will not only help you recover but will also become a source of strength for you as you face future challenges, knowing you have a circle of love and understanding around you.

Friendship is a living thing. It changes shape as you do. Some friends will remain constant, steady companions through every season of your life. Others will fade into the background, not out of conflict but because your paths no longer align. This natural ebb and flow doesn't make the connection any less real. It simply means that not every friendship is meant to last forever.

Healing helps you accept this truth without bitterness. You begin to understand that some people were meant to walk beside you for a chapter, not a lifetime. They helped you grow, helped you survive, helped you remember who you are. Letting go of them means recognizing that you both have new directions to follow.

The friendships that last will start to feel steadier, grounded in trust and mutual respect that has been shaped by experience. You'll begin to see that the people who stay aren't always the ones who make the most noise or show up every day, but they're the ones whose care never wavers. They grow with you instead of holding on to who you used to be. That's how you know they're meant to stay. It's how they continue to meet you where you are now, with understanding and genuine love.

Forgiveness is one of the most underrated parts of friendship, especially while you're healing. It's easy to expect the people you love to always get it right, to say the perfect thing, to understand exactly what you need. When they don't, it can sting and start to build distance between you. Forgiveness keeps that from happening. It lets love stay alive where resentment could have grown. You must remember that everyone, including you, is still learning how to love, how to communicate, and how to show up.

There are also moments when you must forgive yourself for disappearing, for being distant, or for the times when pain made you say things you didn't mean. Healing changes you, and that change can sometimes confuse the people around you. They might not understand this new version of you right away, and that's okay. True friendship makes room for growth and change.

Forgiveness creates space for relationships to evolve instead of falling apart. It lets you honor what once was while still leaving room for what's next. The most meaningful friendships are rarely perfect. They last because both people have learned that compassion matters more than getting everything right and that love has the strength to bend without breaking.

As you think about the role of close friendships, it's also important to remember that all relationships, whether romantic or not, can shape your healing. The people you let close to you influence how safe you feel, how seen you feel, and how you continue to grow. Romantic relationships can add another layer of complexity, especially when one partner doesn't fully understand the emotional weight that trauma carries. Just like friendship, to thrive, these relationships need trust, communication, and respect. The healthiest ones give you space to be yourself while offering stability and care. Whether it's a friend or a partner, the right relationship helps you rebuild the parts of yourself that pain once tried to take away.

Leaning on the right people doesn't follow any single pattern. What you need might look different from what someone else needs, and that's perfectly okay. The key is finding people who can meet you where you are instead of expecting you to be somewhere else. You never have to fix yourself before you're worthy of love and support. The right people will make room for you exactly as you are and help you heal at your own pace. Healing isn't a straight path, and the relationships that help you grow are the ones that understand that truth. They don't rush you or demand that you be further along; they walk with you, steady and patient, every step of the way.

With time, you start to recognize the relationships that feed your soul. These are the people you can lean on fully, knowing their care is genuine and their love is steady. They remind you of your strength when you forget, and they offer kindness without conditions. The more you allow these connections to support you, the more you realize that healing isn't about finding perfect people. It's about finding the ones who stay beside you through every high and low, who help you return to yourself again and again. The road to recovery might be long, but with the right people beside you, it becomes softer, brighter, and so much easier to keep walking.

Chapter 14

Relationships and Renewal

Building Love That Supports Your Healing

At the end of each day, as you reflect on the moments spent with friends and family—laughter filling the room, stories shared, and the simple joy of human connection—you might return home to the person who shares your most intimate space, the one who sees you when you're at your most vulnerable. This person is more than just a romantic partner; they play a unique and often pivotal role in your healing journey. While friends and family members provide essential emotional support, romantic relationships tend to hold a deeper significance in the process of healing. It's within the intimate space of a partnership where the most profound moments of growth, healing, and vulnerability often occur.

However, relationships are not automatic sources of comfort and safety. They are cultivated, nurtured, and require a continuous investment of love, respect, and communication. When you come home to your partner, ideally, that home should feel like a refuge—a place where you can drop the weight of the world and just *be*. Your partner, ideally, should be someone who supports your healing, not adds to your burden. The right person will help you face your struggles with patience, understanding, and care, and not demand that you be someone you are not or expect you to heal faster than is natural.

When you're healing from past pain, especially in the wake of trauma, the pressure to be "whole" can feel overwhelming. Yet, a healthy relationship does not expect one partner to carry the burden of the other's healing. A healthy relationship consists of walking beside each other and creating a space of mutual growth. The healing process can be incredibly personal, and it's important to remember that the right partner will not push you to "move on" from your trauma but will walk with you as you process, reflect, and learn how to carry it with you. A loving partner doesn't seek to change you—they embrace you, brokenness and all. They remind you of your strength, even when you don't see it yourself, and they help you rebuild your sense of self-worth.

The way we attach to others often tells the story of where we have been. It is a reflection of how love once felt in our earliest memories, how safety was offered or withheld, and how connection was taught to us long before we even had words for it. Those early experiences leave imprints that shape how we reach for others and how we protect ourselves. When love once came with conditions or pain, we carry those lessons into adulthood without realizing it. Trauma can leave its fingerprints on these patterns, teaching us to crave closeness while also fearing it. Some people build walls around their hearts to keep hurt out. Others cling tightly, afraid that letting go will mean losing love altogether. Neither reaction is a flaw. Both are ways the heart learned to survive when it was trying to make sense of love and safety in an unpredictable world.

Healing asks you to look at your patterns with understanding rather than judgment. It means noticing the moments when you pull away and the moments when you reach too quickly, and being able to say to yourself, *I understand why I respond this way*. That awareness takes some of the edge off the fear that once dictated your reactions. It creates room for compassion where self-criticism used to take over. Healing often begins in the pause between reacting and reflecting, in the willingness to see your patterns not as flaws but as protective strategies that once made sense.

A supportive partner will not take those moments personally. They will stay steady, offering calm instead of frustration. They will remind you, often without words, that safety can exist even in vulnerability. With time, that steadiness begins to teach your body something new. The alarms that once blared in the presence of closeness begin to quiet. The instinct to brace for disappointment fades a little more with each consistent act of care. Slowly, you start to learn that love does not have to feel unpredictable to be real. It can be quiet. It can be calm. It can feel like coming home to yourself after years of waiting for something to go wrong. Love, in its truest form, becomes the place where you can finally breathe freely, knowing that this time, it is safe to stay.

True intimacy grows when both people understand that attachment is not a test to pass but a bridge to build. It is something you cross together, over and over, until trust feels like second nature. Every honest conversation becomes a step forward. Every gentle response begins to rewrite the story of what love feels like. The more safety you create through small acts of care, the more your heart learns to relax in someone's presence. You no longer mistake chaos for passion or silence for rejection. Instead, you recognize that connection is not something you need to brace yourself for. It is something you are safe to rest in, to receive fully, without apology or fear.

For those not yet in a relationship, this chapter serves as a guide to what to look for when choosing a partner. It's crucial to recognize that a relationship, particularly after you've gone through personal growth or healing, should not be entered into lightly. You must be intentional about who you choose. Seek someone who respects your past but doesn't expect you to remain tethered to it. Find someone who understands that the scars you carry are part of your story, but they do not define you. Choose a partner who encourages your healing and growth, not someone who needs you to stay in a fixed state of pain, just to make them feel comfortable. In short, look for a partner who values the essence of who you are, not just who you are in the moment of struggle.

When you are in a relationship, it is natural to want to retreat inwardly when things get tough, to retreat into yourself to manage your pain. However, one of the most powerful actions you can take is to lean into your partner, not away from them. It's easy to build emotional walls when you're hurting, thinking that you need to protect yourself. Yet, isolation can prevent healing. True intimacy is found when you allow someone into your process, even when it's difficult to share. Being vulnerable doesn't mean laying your entire emotional burden on your partner; it means letting them in to witness your struggles, fears, and emotional turmoil. It's about offering them the opportunity to support you, without expecting them to "fix" you. Vulnerability fosters connection—it allows the other person to show up for you, to understand you more deeply, and to meet you where you are.

After pain, the way you give and receive love rarely stays the same. The things that once made you feel seen or cherished can start to feel unfamiliar, almost foreign. You might find that compliments no longer land the way they used to or that silence suddenly feels safer than attention. What once brought you comfort might now stir discomfort because your heart has learned to protect itself differently. Healing changes the way love moves through you. It teaches you to listen for what your soul actually needs, not just what you used to accept.

You might notice that words of affirmation begin to hold more meaning than grand gestures because they reassure you that love can still speak gently. Or perhaps physical touch, once so natural, feels tender and raw until trust is rebuilt. You are broken or incapable of love, you are learning to love again through a new lens. Healing reshapes your boundaries, your desires, and your definition of intimacy. It invites you to explore what feels safe now, what softens your body, what helps your heart unclench.

This rediscovery is part of the beauty of healing. It gives you permission to build a new language of love—one that honors who you are today, not who you were before the pain. It is the process of relearning what comfort feels like, how safety sounds, and what genuine connection looks like when it is not laced with fear. Through patience and self-awareness, you begin to open again, slowly, bravely, in your own time. Love after healing feels different, but it also feels truer. It comes from a place of choice rather than survival, and it becomes something you can finally trust to stay.

Communicating these needs takes courage, especially when your voice still trembles from old memories of not being heard. It can feel unnatural at first to say, "I need more reassurance," or "I need space when I'm upset," when your past taught you that silence was safer. Yet this kind of honesty is what clears the fog between two people. The right partner won't treat your needs as too much or too complicated. They will listen, not to fix or defend but to understand. They will hold space for your words and show you through their actions that love can be steady even when you're not. When both people take the time to learn how the other gives and receives love, connection begins to flow naturally. It no longer feels like guessing or walking on eggshells. It starts to feel like home.

Healing within love means realizing that asking for care does not make you needy—it makes you human. It is an act of honesty, not weakness. It takes strength to say, "I need you right now," or "I'm not okay today." It means trusting that your partner can hold what you share without judgment. True love can handle truth. It doesn't shrink when you show your emotions. Instead, it grows stronger because vulnerability becomes a shared language of understanding. When both people speak from that place of openness, love becomes a dialogue, not a performance.

Self-care, self-awareness, and independence are the roots of any healthy partnership. Healing requires both inner work and shared effort. Your partner can walk beside you, but they cannot carry your wounds for you. What they can do is stay with you while you face them. The most nurturing relationships honor this balance. They make space for your growth while also tending to their own. Both people learn to share the emotional weight, to care for each other without losing themselves, and to build a bond strong enough to hold two whole, evolving hearts.

In a healing relationship, there will be times when one partner takes on a heavier emotional load than the other. There's no shame in this, but it's essential to recognize when you're leaning too heavily on your partner or when you need to step up for them. This reciprocal support is what makes a relationship strong—it's about the waves of caring for each other, understanding when one person needs more, and knowing when to give space. At the same time, it's crucial to communicate openly about how you feel and what you need. One of the most common mistakes people make is expecting their partner to read their minds. Communication is key, especially when healing from trauma. Share your emotional landscape and invite your partner to do the same. These conversations create an environment where both people can thrive.

If you cannot speak openly with your partner about your emotions, needs, or concerns without fearing their reaction, that is a serious warning sign. A relationship should not require you to filter yourself in order to stay safe. You should be able to express discomfort, ask for reassurance, or clarify expectations without anticipating anger, withdrawal, or punishment. If honest conversation feels risky, the issue is not simply communication skills; it is safety. Emotional openness cannot exist where fear is present. If you find yourself consistently holding back to avoid conflict or protect the other person's ego, that dynamic needs to be addressed. You cannot heal in this environment. Open dialogue is not optional in a healthy relationship. It is foundational.

When you have lived through pain, it can become automatic to manage the emotions around you before you acknowledge your own. You may catch yourself scanning for tension, analyzing your partner's tone, or adjusting your words to keep the peace. You become the steady one, the reasonable one, the one who absorbs discomfort so it does not escalate. On the surface, that can look like maturity or kindness. Underneath, it is often survival. You learned that stabilizing others helped stabilize your environment.

Over time, that constant regulation has a cost. It drains you gradually, until you feel exhausted and stressed without a clear reason. You may find that you offer reassurance easily but hesitate to ask for it. You show up for others without pause, yet struggle to express when you need support. At some point, you realize you have been managing two emotional worlds when you were only responsible for your own.

Healthy love requires balance. You are not meant to hold the emotional world of two people on your shoulders. A real partnership invites both people to show up fully, to tend to their own emotions and still have enough strength left to care for each other. That kind of balance builds stability. It creates a home where both can rest without fear that everything will fall apart if one person finally takes a breath. When both partners take responsibility for their own emotional well-being, love becomes a shared effort rather than a constant test of endurance.

Love should never feel like a job you cannot step away from. It should feel like an easy rhythm that moves between you, a steady flow of giving and receiving. Some days you might carry more, and other days your partner will, but over time it evens out. When emotional labor is mutual, it becomes a language of trust. You get to feel safe in each other's care. You get to exhale. That is when love feels like partnership instead of performance, when it nourishes instead of depletes, and when it starts to feel like something that can truly last.

While emotional support is fundamental, it's also essential that a nurturing relationship becomes a space for joy and love, not just survival. Yes, healing is hard work, and some days will feel like trudging through mud, but there should be moments of lightness, fun, and connection. Healing doesn't mean living in a constant state of seriousness or sadness. Laugh, create memories, go on dates, and engage in activities that bring both of you joy. The balance of pain and joy is a cornerstone of a healthy partnership, and these moments of connection remind you both that healing doesn't mean you need to put life on hold. There's still room for love, excitement, and playfulness.

Your healing journey might lead to many changes within you and your relationship. That's to be expected. Personal growth and healing are not static. As you grow, your needs, desires, and even boundaries might evolve. The key here is that you and your partner grow together. Regular check-ins and open communication help keep this dynamic intact. Discuss your evolving needs, check in on how each person feels, and reevaluate your relationship goals. Creating space for these conversations helps ensure that the relationship continues to be a source of strength for both of you. These aren't just conversations about what's going wrong—they're also about what's going right and how you can keep cultivating love and support in a way that meets the needs of both partners.

The most meaningful love will not only comfort you, but it will also invite you to grow. It holds up a mirror and asks you to face yourself with honesty and patience. The right partner will see both your strengths and your blind spots and will encourage you to meet both with compassion.

Growth within love is not always graceful. It can feel unsettling at times because it calls you to pay attention to your habits, your fears, your patterns, and your reactions. It asks you to stay open even when you would rather turn away. Healing within love means seeing yourself clearly without judgment, learning from what surfaces, and realizing that love can expand through truth just as much as through tenderness.

A loving partner will never ask you to change to please them. They will remind you that you are already enough while still encouraging you to reach for your potential. They will ask thoughtful questions that make you pause and reflect on what you want, what you need, and who you are becoming. When you doubt yourself, they will speak to the version of you that already exists beneath the uncertainty. Love that nurtures growth does not stay still. It adapts, deepens, and matures over time. It moves with you, growing steadier as you evolve, guiding you toward what is next instead of keeping you tied to what feels safe or familiar.

When love challenges you, it is not asking you to perform or prove your worth. It is inviting you to rise. It pushes you to listen to your intuition, to practice honesty, and to trust yourself enough to change. The kind of partner who helps you grow is not someone who tries to fix you but someone who stands beside you as you uncover who you are meant to be. They celebrate your evolution because they see that your healing and your becoming are part of the beauty of loving you. Through that kind of love, you learn that growth does not take you away from love. It deepens it.

Growth in a relationship should never require you to become someone unrecognizable to yourself. You cannot force your partner to change, and they cannot force you. Real change is voluntary. It happens when a person takes responsibility for their own patterns and chooses to evolve.

A healthy relationship does not revolve around molding one another into preferred versions. It allows space for development without erasing identity. If you feel pressured to shrink, reshape, or abandon core parts of yourself to maintain connection, something is misaligned. Love should support refinement, not replacement. You should feel more like yourself as you grow, not less.

While vulnerability and emotional honesty are vital, it's equally important to nurture trust. Trust is built through consistent actions and genuine care over time. When a partner is committed to the relationship, they show up for you—not just when things are easy but especially when they're hard. Trust is built through shared experiences, through the act of showing up for each other consistently. If either partner feels unsafe, unheard, or unvalued, the trust within the relationship erodes. As you work on healing, take the time to foster trust by being transparent, being reliable, and showing your commitment to nurturing both yourself and your relationship.

Every relationship encounters misunderstanding. No matter how strong the connection, there will be moments when words land wrong or silence carries more weight than intended. Healing does not mean preventing those moments. It means learning how to respond to them with honesty and restraint instead of defensiveness. Repair is what sustains love over time. It happens after tension, when both people decide to address what occurred rather than avoid it.

Repair requires humility. It involves saying, "I was wrong," or "I misunderstood," and taking responsibility without qualification. It asks you to lower your guard long enough to see the person in front of you clearly, not as an adversary but as someone you value. Choosing repair over pride is what allows trust to strengthen rather than erode.

When you begin to care more about connection than about being right, healing starts to take place in the moments that matter most. It begins in the pause before you speak, in the deep breath that keeps you from saying something you cannot take back, in the softness that returns after pride starts to fade. The apology becomes more than a word. It becomes an open door back to closeness, an invitation to say, "I still choose you, even in this." It is no longer about who was wrong or who caused the hurt. It is about how you choose to find your way back to each other.

When each person takes responsibility for their part, even the small moments that went unnoticed before, trust begins to rebuild itself. You start to see that love does not crumble when tested. It becomes stronger because you both cared enough to protect it. Every act of repair, no matter how small, sends a message that your relationship can survive tension, that it can weather discomfort, and that what you share is far more important than winning the argument.

Repair reinforces that love is not fragile. It can withstand honesty, frustration, and imperfection without unraveling. Love does not require perfection to endure, but it does require intention. It requires two people who are willing to return to the conversation when it would be easier to withdraw.

Healing within a relationship often happens in ordinary moments, when both people choose care over distance and understanding over pride. Each return to the table strengthens the foundation. Each repaired misunderstanding adds stability rather than erosion. Over time, love shifts from being an idea or a promise to being a practice. It shows up in daily decisions to engage, to listen, and to protect the connection. Real love is not sustained by flawlessness but by consistent effort.

Healing from trauma often asks you to walk through layers of yourself that you once had to hide. It is emotional work that reaches into places you thought you had already left behind. Some days it will feel heavy, as if your heart is carrying more than it can hold. There will be moments when your emotions come rushing to the surface without warning, when memories feel too close, and when you wonder if you will ever feel completely free from the past. The right partner will never rush you through that process or make you feel like your pain is inconvenient. They will hold space for you to be honest about what you feel, even when it is hard to articulate. They will listen without trying to fix you. They will sit in the quiet with you when words are too much and remind you, through their steady presence, that you are not alone.

In time, they will gently encourage you to keep moving forward, not because they are tired of your healing but because they believe in your ability to grow beyond what once hurt you. At the same time, healing within love is not a one-sided effort. It is just as important to make sure your partner feels seen, valued, and understood. You cannot pour endlessly without replenishing the connection between you. Your partner is not meant to be your outlet for anger or your shield against every difficult emotion, just as you are not meant to carry the full weight of theirs. Love requires balance. It thrives in mutual care, where both hearts are tended to with gentleness.

It is also important not to use your partner as a container for every surge of emotion that trauma brings up. They can support you, but they are not responsible for absorbing unprocessed anger or enduring repeated outbursts without acknowledgment. Being triggered does not give you permission to disregard their experience. If you recognize that your pain has spilled over in ways that were unfair, it is your responsibility to own it. That may mean offering a direct apology or expressing appreciation for their patience. Self-awareness matters here. Healing does not excuse harmful behavior. It requires accountability alongside vulnerability. When both people feel respected, the relationship remains a place of support rather than strain.

Healing from trauma asks for patience, humility, and grace rather than perfection. It is the willingness to keep showing up for yourself and for each other, even when it feels uncomfortable. As you do the work of untangling your own pain, it is equally important to honor your partner's emotional needs. Love deepens when both partners feel safe enough to be imperfect together. When that safety is present, even the hard days become part of the healing, not setbacks.

One of the hardest fears to face in love is the fear of being left. Even when you are with someone steady and kind, that fear can live beneath the surface. It whispers in moments of silence and makes you question if good things can last. You might catch yourself watching for signs that the connection is fading or rehearsing heartbreak before it happens. You might find yourself bracing for disappointment, as if preparing for loss could somehow make it hurt less. This fear does not mean you are ungrateful or damaged. It means your heart remembers what it felt like to be unsafe. It remembers the nights you had to be your own comfort, the times love disappeared without explanation, and the exhaustion of pretending you were fine.

That memory is carried in the body, not just in thought. It can surface when someone treats you with steady care, because safety may feel unfamiliar if you have been conditioned for survival. The first step in easing that fear is recognizing it for what it is. It was a protective response that once made sense, even if it no longer fits your present circumstances. It deserves understanding, not shame.

When you can acknowledge the fear without allowing it to dictate your behavior, you create room for intimacy. A healthy partner will respond to that fear with patience rather than irritation. Their consistency becomes evidence that not every connection ends in loss. Over time, the fear loses intensity. It no longer dictates your reactions. Gradually, you begin to trust that love can remain, and that you are safe enough to settle into it.

Healing that fear takes time, reassurance, and steady proof that love can stay. It grows through the quiet consistency of small, trustworthy moments. A returned message. A boundary that is honored. A promise that is kept without needing to be reminded. Each act of reliability helps your body relax a little more. It teaches you that safety is not an illusion, that love can be both passionate and dependable. The right partner will never tell you to simply move on from your fear. They will understand that healing requires presence, not pressure. They will stay patient, showing through their steadiness that they are not going anywhere.

As time passes, the fear that once held your heart begins to loosen its grip. The nights spent overthinking soften into something gentler. You begin to realize that you no longer live in a constant state of waiting for goodbye. You stop scanning every silence for hidden meaning or preparing yourself for loss before it ever arrives. Instead, your attention starts to shift toward what is real and present. You notice the warmth of a quiet evening, the comfort of a familiar voice, the way safety feels when it finally stops feeling temporary.

Love becomes something you can lean into without holding your breath. It no longer feels like something fragile that might break under the weight of your hope. It becomes a steady, grounding presence that whispers to you again and again that it is safe to stay, rest, and be loved.

Love is a feeling, but it is also a choice. It is the decision to stay engaged when conflict would make it easier to withdraw. It is the willingness to work through misunderstandings instead of abandoning the connection at the first sign of discomfort. It is choosing to get back up after disappointment, to compromise when necessary, and to show up with intention rather than impulse. Feelings may ebb and shift, but the choice to remain committed is what gives love its stability.

Not every relationship that claims to be healing truly is. Sometimes two people find each other in their pain and mistake that recognition for destiny. The connection can feel electric, almost magnetic, yet what you are really feeling is familiarity. It mirrors your wounds instead of your growth. You might confuse chaos for passion, mistaking the highs and lows for depth. But beneath that intensity, there is often the same cycle of anxiety, guilt, and uncertainty you once tried to escape.

Love that leaves you restless is not healing love. True healing love feels different. It does not demand constant proof of loyalty or devotion. It feels calm and steady. It allows you to exhale. It gives you room to expand, to become the version of yourself that was always waiting to emerge once you were finally safe. Healing love will not hold you back out of fear. It will encourage your becoming, even if it means growing beyond what you once thought love had to be.

Love does not require you to shrink in order to maintain it. If you have to silence your needs, suppress your growth, or manage someone else's insecurity to keep the relationship intact, the dynamic is not healthy. Control can sometimes present itself as protection or devotion, but its effect is constriction. When a relationship consistently leaves you anxious, depleted, or questioning your value, that pattern deserves examination. Love should not demand that you compromise your well-being to preserve the connection. It should support both the relationship and the individuals within it.

Healthy love does not punish boundaries or interpret independence as rejection. It allows space for a voice, for preferences, for growth. It does not require you to remain in the version of yourself that was shaped by past wounds. It supports forward movement. Partnership is not about dissolving into a single identity. It is about two distinct people choosing to move alongside one another with mutual respect. If the relationship begins to feel defined by guilt, confusion, or chronic imbalance, stepping back is not selfish. It is a way of restoring perspective. Clarity allows you to evaluate whether the connection strengthens your stability or erodes it. Peace should not be earned through endurance. It should be preserved through alignment.

It is important to remember that no one person is meant to be your everything. Expecting that will only lead to exhaustion for both of you. Healthy love exists within a larger circle of connection. Friends, family, mentors, and even your relationship with yourself all form a web of support that keeps you grounded. The stronger the web is, the stronger your relationship becomes. When both partners are supported by having a life outside the partnership, love feels lighter. It is built no longer on dependency but on choice. You stay not because you have to but because you genuinely want to. That is what creates a love that grows instead of consumes, a love that strengthens you rather than empties you.

Lastly, remember that healing is not a finish line you cross one day and declare complete. It is a lifelong unfolding, a path that keeps changing shape as you do. There will be seasons when it feels effortless and others when it feels like you are starting over. A loving partner will not expect you to always be strong or certain. They will stand beside you through it all. They will see your wounds without turning away, listen to the stories behind your pain, and love you not in spite of them but through them. Real love does not flinch at the messiness of growth. It holds space for it, reminding you that you are not too much to be loved as you are. Through that kind of love, you begin to find a deeper peace, not just within the relationship but within yourself. You start to see that healing and love can coexist, that being loved well can help you see yourself in a softer, truer light.

When you have a partner who stays with you through the uncertain parts, the journey feels less lonely. You begin to see beauty even in the moments that once made you afraid. The hard days no longer define you; they remind you that you are still learning, still growing, still capable of love. A relationship rooted in trust, communication, and respect can become a sanctuary where both people heal together. It becomes a place where you can fall apart and rebuild, where laughter returns after the tears, and where hope quietly settles back into your life.

Chapter 15

Growth through Healing
The Journey from Pain to Peace

Healing from trauma is an immense ongoing journey, one that doesn't have a clear-cut timeline or straightforward path. There are so many steps involved, and each step can feel overwhelming. At times, it might seem like you're taking two steps forward and one step back. But despite the challenges, it is possible to rebuild yourself from the ground up, one piece at a time. Trauma doesn't disappear; it leaves a mark on your life, sometimes in ways you don't even realize. However, by allowing yourself the space to heal and grow, you can gradually make progress and create a future that's not defined by what you've been through. Healing is not about erasing the scars but learning to live with them so they no longer control you.

Trauma, when it strikes, can feel like a crushing weight that shatters the sense of safety and stability we once knew. It can lead us to question our worth, our ability to trust others, and the very foundation of our identity. In some cases, trauma can set us on a path of doom, where the pain becomes the lens through which we see the world. The haunting memories, the constant fear, and the feeling of being trapped in the aftermath can make it seem like there's no way out. It's easy to feel lost in the shadows, to wonder if you'll ever emerge from the darkness.

What many don't realize, though, is that within trauma lies the seed of transformation, the potential for deep, profound growth. Trauma is not just an experience to survive—it is an opportunity to rebuild and redefine your life in ways you never thought possible. The choice between doom and growth lies in our ability to process, accept, and ultimately redefine what has happened to us.

Trauma doesn't need to be a life sentence; it can be a catalyst for a new chapter, one where resilience is built, wisdom is gained, and strength is forged. It is through the pain that we often find the most profound strength. Choosing growth requires courage—courage to face the pain, to sit with the discomfort, and to be willing to see beyond the hurt. It means embracing the vulnerability of acknowledging your wounds but not allowing them to define who you are. Instead, you become the one who reclaims their power, who learns to turn their pain into a wellspring of wisdom.

Healing invites you to gather the parts of yourself that were scattered by pain. Every version of you—the one who survived, the one who struggled, and the one who still dares to hope—belongs to your story. You are a mosaic made from every moment you have lived, and your beauty lies in that complexity. When you begin to see those pieces as fragments of strength instead of reminders of what was lost, you start to understand what wholeness truly feels like. Healing lets you see your life as an artist sees a canvas, recognizing how even the darkest shades add depth to the picture. The cracks do not ruin it. They make it real. They are proof that you have lived and continued on, even when life broke you open.

There will be times when you resist certain parts of yourself, especially the ones that remind you of fear or regret. You might catch yourself avoiding memories of choices that hurt you or the moments when you stayed somewhere too long. It can be tempting to judge those versions of yourself, to wish you could rewrite their story. Yet healing invites you to reach back and hold their hand. It asks you to understand that they were trying to survive with the knowledge they had then.

Those moments you wish you could erase often hold the clearest lessons about courage, endurance, and growth. Sit with them. Listen to what they are trying to tell you. The pain might soften when you do. You begin to see that even the parts of you formed in hardship have value. They taught you resilience. They helped you learn who you are and what you now refuse to become again.

Wholeness does not come from perfection. It comes from acceptance. It is the peace that forms when you can live in your own skin without flinching away from any part of yourself. It is the ability to look at who you are today and feel at ease rather than conflicted. Nothing about you needs to be erased for you to deserve peace. Healing allows you to stop performing for approval and rest in the truth that you are already enough. When you stop separating the parts of yourself into what you love and what you hide, your life begins to feel lighter. You stop fighting your reflection and begin to see it as a testament to everything you have survived.

A crucial step in this journey is to reframe the narrative you tell yourself. Instead of identifying as a victim of trauma, begin to see yourself as a survivor—someone who has endured, who is still standing. Celebrate small victories along the way: a day when you feel more present, an hour when the pain doesn't consume you, a moment when you realize you've made it through a difficult situation feeling stronger than before. These incremental shifts are signs of growth, and they're not to be overlooked. Over time, these small changes accumulate into something more powerful: a life lived with resilience, wisdom, and grace.

For a long time, survival might have been your only goal. You learned how to read every situation like a map of potential danger, how to move through your days while keeping the most fragile parts of yourself hidden. You became skilled at scanning for threats, both seen and unseen, always ready to protect yourself from what might come next. Survival trained you to stay alert, to make yourself small when needed, to keep going no matter how much it hurt. That kind of strength is remarkable, but it also comes at a cost. It can keep you locked in patterns of vigilance long after the danger has passed. Healing begins when you start to loosen that grip, when you finally whisper to yourself that it's safe to rest. It's in that quiet permission that your body and spirit begin to remember what living feels like.

The first signs of this transformation often appear when you least expect them. It might happen on a morning when you wake up and realize your first feeling isn't fear. It might be the sound of your own laughter, unguarded and real, filling a room that once held only silence. You start to notice the world around you in new ways—the way sunlight softens through the window, the scent of coffee, the warmth of clean sheets against your skin. You start to notice that you are breathing more freely. Life begins to show you its colors again in the gentle rhythm of ordinary moments. Slowly, the world stops feeling like a place to endure and starts feeling like a place to inhabit. That is the quiet beauty of healing: it teaches you to see life again, not through fear, but through curiosity.

Start by practicing self-compassion. Healing might begin as an inward process, but it never stays contained there. Each act of gentleness toward yourself sends out a ripple, touching everything and everyone around you. When you speak to yourself with patience instead of judgment, you begin to notice how the world responds differently. The tone of your voice softens. Your presence feels steadier. The chaos that once surrounded you starts to fade.

Those closest to you can sense the change before you even name it. They see it in your calm expression, in the way you no longer rush to defend or prove yourself, in the quiet steadiness that follows you into a room. Your healing teaches others that peace is found through acceptance. You become a living example of what it means to carry grace in your own skin.

The ripple of your healing shows itself in unexpected ways. A friend feels comfortable enough to share something tender because they sense you will truly listen. A relative speaks more softly around you because they recognize that you move differently through the world now. Even strangers can feel it—a smile exchanged at the grocery store, a small moment of kindness that lightens someone's day without you even realizing it.

Healing changes your energy. It alters the way you see and interact with others. You begin to understand that your peace is not just for you. It becomes something that lifts the people around you, creating small openings for connection and relief.

As your healing deepens, your growth becomes a kind of revolution. It happens not through rebellion but through presence. You model boundaries that are firm yet compassionate. You take accountability without collapsing into shame. You show that real strength is steady and kind. When others witness you choosing calm over conflict, or grace over control, it gives them permission to do the same. They begin to see that peace is not weakness and that healing is not selfish.

Each time you respond with understanding rather than fear, you help the world soften a little. You begin to change the emotional climate of your surroundings simply by existing as someone who has done the inner work. Healing might begin as something personal, but its reach extends far beyond you. It becomes a force of influence, transforming not only your life but the lives you touch with every step forward.

It's easy to blame yourself or feel guilty for not healing faster, but recovery takes time. Be gentle with yourself. Allow yourself to mourn what was lost and to acknowledge the depth of your pain. Your grief is valid, and it deserves the space to be expressed. In healing, there are no timelines; there is only your journey. Instead of rushing yourself through the process, embrace each stage—no matter how difficult—knowing that it is part of the greater whole.

There is a particular kind of bravery in beginning again. It is the courage to step forward, even when you know life might bruise you once more, and still trust that you will find your way through if it does. Beginning again is rarely marked by grand moments or sweeping change. It often begins in the quietest acts of faith. It looks like buying fresh flowers for your kitchen table because you want to see something beautiful in your space. It looks like opening the curtains and letting the sunlight spill into a room that once felt too heavy to enter. It looks like signing up for a class, calling a friend, or simply deciding to get out of bed when you do not feel ready.

These moments might seem small, but they carry the power to shift everything. Each one says, "I am still here." Each one plants a seed of renewal, even before you can see it growing.

To begin again is to trust that life still holds something meaningful for you. It is to recognize that your story is still unfolding and that the pages ahead do not have to mirror the ones behind. Beginning again requires you to open your heart to the idea that love, peace, and purpose can return in forms you never expected. It asks you to believe that there is still joy waiting to find you.

Every sunrise becomes an invitation to try again, to take one more step toward the life you are rebuilding.

As healing continues, you might begin to experience a shift in how you relate to the world around you. You'll feel a sense of freedom you didn't know was possible, a kind of peace that isn't dependent on external circumstances. The heavy burden of the past will start to feel lighter. Your heart will open, and you might find yourself more empathetic, more understanding of others who are going through their own struggles. Trauma might have happened to you, but it does not define who you are.

Building trust again can be one of the most challenging yet transformative aspects of healing. Whether it's trust in yourself, in others, or in the world around you, the process of rebuilding trust is gradual. It's not something you can rush, and it takes intentional effort. Rebuilding trust with yourself might mean learning to listen to your own needs and desires again or rediscovering your ability to make decisions without fear. Rebuilding trust in others might involve setting healthy boundaries, taking risks in small steps, and allowing people to prove themselves to you over time. Above all, know that trust is not a given—it must be earned, nurtured, and protected. By choosing to trust again, even in small ways, you give yourself permission to experience life more fully and to step out of the shadows that trauma casts.

When you reach a point of healing, you'll feel a sense of completion. This doesn't mean the pain is gone entirely but rather that it no longer controls you. You'll have grown stronger, wiser, and more attuned to your own needs and desires.

Healing will feel like coming home to yourself—a rediscovery of who you truly are without the weight of past hurts. You'll have created a life from the ashes of your trauma, and in that life, you'll find peace, connection, and the freedom to be who you were always meant to be. You'll know that no matter what happens, you are resilient, and you can continue to grow.

Healing requires clarity, much like water must be clean before it can brew the perfect cup of coffee. Imagine your life as a carafe waiting to be filled. What you pour into it determines the quality of what comes out. If the water is murky, the coffee will always taste off, no matter how beautiful the mug or how expensive the beans. In the same way, when your heart and mind are clouded by unresolved pain, everything you build will carry a trace of that heaviness. You might move through the motions of life and create things that look whole from the outside yet still feel something missing within.

Healing asks you to pause long enough to look at what you are carrying and decide whether it is time to let some of it go. That moment of stillness, uncomfortable as it might be, becomes the first step toward true restoration.

Your mind starts to clear when you stop distracting yourself from what needs attention. Sit in silence with your own thoughts. Allow memories that you have avoided surface. Speak the truth out loud. These moments require bravery because they ask you to look directly at what has shaped you.

Without that clarity, even the most polished life will begin to feel hollow. You can fill your days with success, with beauty, with things that sparkle under the right light, but if your pain remains unhealed, it will eventually rise to the surface. It might show up as restlessness, exhaustion, or the nagging sense that something is missing.

Healing happens when you choose to face the truth and cleanse what has been clouding your inner world. When you give yourself the space to feel and rebuild, your life begins to taste different. It becomes richer, steadier, and more genuine. Just as clear water brings out the true flavor of coffee, clarity allows you to create a life that nourishes you from the inside out.

In the same way, your healing should start with self-love and self-care. Before you can pour into others, you must ensure that you're filling yourself up. Take time to nurture yourself, to understand your needs, and to honor your emotions. Your healing journey is yours alone, but you don't have to walk it by yourself. Surround yourself with supportive people—friends, family, or a partner—who can provide the love and encouragement you need to move forward. These are your resources, your source of clarity and strength, helping you to gather the "clear water" necessary for your healing.

When you allow yourself to heal, to become the best version of yourself, you create a life that's worth living, one that radiates positivity and joy to everyone around you.

In addition to nurturing yourself, take time to forgive—both others and yourself. Forgiving others for their actions doesn't mean condoning their behavior; it means freeing yourself from the emotional chains that keep you bound to the past. Similarly, forgiving yourself is essential to healing. Don't blame yourself for the way things happened or for your perceived failures in the healing process. Let go of that weight so that you can fully step into your power and embrace the freedom to move forward.

Your healing carries more weight than you realize. Every choice you make in how you move forward becomes a kind of map for someone else who is still lost in their pain. You might not notice it, but the way you speak, listen, and carry yourself teaches others what healing can look like in real life.

Your patience shows them that growth takes time. Your gentleness shows them that softness and strength can belong in the same person. The grace you extend to yourself becomes a living example of what grace truly means. You are showing others that healing is not a performance or a straight path but a daily practice of choosing peace even when it would be easier to choose bitterness.

Each healed action becomes a quiet kind of teaching. When you stand firm in your boundaries, you remind others that self-respect and compassion can coexist. When you speak your truth without anger, you show that authenticity can thrive even in the aftermath of betrayal. Every time you forgive, every time you choose patience or courage, you create ripples that reach further than you can see.

These choices might seem small in the moment, but they are what transform healing into legacy. You are proving that love can still be chosen after heartbreak, that peace can still be pursued after pain, and that strength can be both steady and kind. In this way, healing becomes more than something you experience. It becomes something you give.

Your legacy does not have to be grand or loud to matter. It can exist in the ways you move through your days: the calm tone you use when comforting someone in pain, the tenderness in the way you parent, the grace in how you carry yourself even when no one is watching.

You remind others that brokenness is not the final chapter of a life, only a turning point. Through your example, you offer proof that something beautiful can rise from what was once shattered. That is the power of healing—it creates something enduring, something that outlives the pain and turns your story into a source of hope for others who are still learning how to begin.

Ultimately, healing is a journey of progress, not perfection. It's about becoming the person you're meant to be, a person who loves and honors themselves. Be patient with yourself. Take things one sip at a time, knowing that every small step you take is leading you toward a better, brighter future. Drink deeply from the well of your own healing, and let that nourish you as you begin to build a life that's filled with hope, strength, and the capacity to thrive.

One day, you might realize that peace has become your natural state. The chaos that once filled your mind no longer feels familiar. You breathe without effort, speak without tension, rest without guilt. This doesn't mean you'll never feel pain again, but pain no longer dictates the rhythm of your life. You begin to respond instead of reacting, to trust instead of brace for impact.

When peace begins to guide you, everything changes. You move through the world more slowly, more intentionally. You become thoughtful about what and who you allow into your space. You start protecting your energy the way you would protect something fragile and precious. Conversations that once drained you no longer hold your attention. You begin to choose calm over chaos, depth over distraction, and presence over performance. Your days take on a gentler pace, one that allows you to actually feel your life as it unfolds. The storms still come, but they do not consume you. You can sit through the thunder and know that the sky will clear again. You have become your own anchor, steady and grounded, no longer defined by the things that once tried to break you.

At the end of the journey, you find yourself circling back to the very beginning, only now you understand it differently. Healing does not take you to some faraway version of yourself. It brings you home. The person you have been searching for was never gone; they were only hidden beneath the weight of fear and survival. When you begin to strip away those layers, you uncover the essence of who you have always been—the part that still knows how to trust, how to feel, how to love. That rediscovery is both tender and powerful. It is the moment you realize that nothing was ever missing from you; it was only waiting to be remembered.

Coming home to yourself does not erase what has been lived. It gives new meaning to it. The memories that once made you ache begin to shift, becoming reminders of how much you have endured. The pain that once hollowed you out becomes the ground from which your strength now grows. The moments of loss that once felt like endings begin to reveal themselves as quiet teachers. Even the scars you carry start to look different. They speak no longer of damage but of survival. They are the visible proof that you have walked through fire and still have something beautiful to show for it.

Healing was never about creating a new version of you. It was about uncovering the truth of who you have always been beneath the noise, beneath the fear, beneath the versions of yourself you built just to get through the day. In that remembering, you find peace that cannot be shaken, freedom that does not rely on circumstance, and a love that cannot be taken from you because it lives inside you now.

This is where your story begins again. You no longer move through life searching for pieces of yourself in other people or places. You have gathered them all and brought them home. You know now that peace is not a destination waiting somewhere in the distance but a state of being you create with every choice to stay true to yourself.

This chapter of your life feels different. It feels honest. You can breathe here. You can rest here. You can look at who you are and feel proud of the person who made it through. The journey brought you back to yourself, and in doing so, it gave you everything you were searching for all along. You have returned to your own heart. You are home.

Afterword

If you've made it to this part of the book, thank you. Truly. Whether you read every chapter or skipped around to the ones that spoke to you, I'm grateful you gave this book space in your life. It's been a long road getting here.

I started writing *Water before Coffee* six years ago, not because I thought I had answers but because I was desperate to find some. At the time, I was nearing the end of the long, messy process of healing from things I never expected to survive—sexual assault, domestic violence, health trauma, mourning the death of a close friend, and even an attempted abduction. I don't write those words lightly. For a long time, I didn't write them at all. I pretended they weren't real. They sat in the corners of my life, irritatingly shaping how I moved through the world, how I saw myself, how safe I felt in my own body and my own home. And let me tell you, I was fantastic at convincing everyone around me that I was perfectly fine.

When I first started trying to heal, I had no idea what I was doing. When these things happen, you don't get handed a checklist on how to process them. I didn't even have the right words for what I was feeling. I had to go searching—for podcasts, books, posts, conversations, groups, professionals—anything that could make me feel less alone. Anything that helped me understand why everything suddenly felt so loud or so numb and why I couldn't bring myself to move forward. I kept wishing there was one place I could go. One book that laid it out plainly and spoke to me like a human. I never found it, so I decided to write it.

These fifteen chapters are the exact things I found myself wrestling with the most. They're the core pieces of what kept coming up again and again, no matter how much time passed. Some days I felt strong and steady, and others I'd spiral right back into old thought patterns. That's part of why it took so many years to write this. I didn't want to give you something surface-level or rushed; I wanted to write from a place of honesty. To say the things I wish someone had said to me.

Writing this book meant revisiting pain I wanted to forget, but it also meant making something meaningful out of it. If you're somewhere on your own healing journey—whether it's brand-new or years deep—I hope this book gave you something useful. I hope it reminded you that your reactions make sense, that your progress doesn't need to look impressive, that your story is still yours, even if other people tried to take it from you or minimize it.

Thank you for spending time with these pages. I didn't write this to be a guidebook or a list of rules. I wrote it as a companion, a hand on your shoulder, something solid to return to when everything feels like too much.

Take what you need from it. Leave the rest. Pick it back up again when life throws you another monkey wrench.

With love,

Melissa Renee

Acknowledgements

There are very few things in life we do alone. This book is no exception.

To my sweet husband, thank you for standing beside me through all six years of this journey. You celebrated every small accomplishment as if it were the finish line. You never blinked at what it cost to bring this book to life. You were the shoulder I cried on when revisiting these memories felt heavier than I expected. You have been my steady support, my safe place, and my clearest example of what healing can look like in real time. Thank you for loving me with all that I carry and for choosing a life with me that made space for my growth.

To my mom, my first and loudest supporter, thank you for cheering me on before I knew what I was building. Your excitement, your pride, and your stack of 10+ preordered copies mean more than I can say. You have always believed that my dreams were worth pursuing.

To my dad, thank you for being the steady voice of truth in my life. You never softened what I needed to hear, and because of that, I learned how to stand on my own. You taught me that I was capable of solving my problems and strong enough to face what was hard.

To my best friend, Melissa, who has known me since I was five years old, thank you for witnessing every chapter of my life. You saw the trauma, the aftermath, and the rebuilding. Thank you for rescuing me from my own mind whenever I needed saving and for reminding me who I am when I forget.

To the experiences that shaped me, even the painful ones, thank you for the strength and awareness they forced me to develop. I would not be the same without them.

To espresso and rock music, thank you for helping me push through the long nights, the rewrites, and the doubt. You carried me more times than I can count.

To the nonfiction authors who brave this genre with honesty and courage, thank you for inspiring me. Your willingness to write the hard truths made it easier for me to write mine.

And finally, to the readers holding this book, thank you for trusting me with your time and your story. I hope these pages meet you exactly where you are.